Fashion
Design
Research

Ezinma
Mbonu

LAURENCE KING

Published in 2014 by
Laurence King Publishing Ltd
361–363 City Road, London,
EC1V 1LR, United Kingdom
T + 44 (0)20 7841 6900
F + 44 (0)20 7841 6910
enquiries@laurenceking.com
www.laurenceking.com

This book was produced by
Laurence King Publishing Ltd, London

A catalogue record for this book is
available from the British Library

ISBN: 978-1-78067-179-6

Design by Jane Chipchase

Printed in China

Front cover (front to back): © LKP, photo by Hayley Bradshaw,
courtesy Meagan S. E. Wellman; © LKP, photo by Hayley
Bradshaw, courtesy Hefina Hedd Williams; Courtesy Ruth Green;
© LKP, photo courtesy Mark Glasgow

Back cover (top to bottom): Courtesy Alice Overington; © LKP,
photo by Hayley Bradshaw, courtesy Meagan S. E. Wellman

Fashion
Design
Research

Ezinma
Mbonu

Laurence King Publishing

Contents

Introduction

Research is essential to fashion design. Innovative design is the result of strong investigative research undertakings. The intention of this book is to unpack the research process by focusing on the core elements that you will need to engage with as a fashion student to ensure that you develop your ideas creatively and thoroughly. Through the research process, you create the building blocks needed to develop a concept. This book shows you how to fully explore and build upon an initial idea through a variety of research methods. In this divergent and expansive first stage, primary, secondary, colour, fabric and market research is undertaken, giving you a well-informed position from which to develop your concept with a deeper level of understanding and subsequent application.

Chapter 1: What is Research? examines the concept of research, and clarifies the difference between primary and secondary research, noting the benefits of both. Getting underway on a brief can often prove quite challenging, so Chapter 2: How to Start Researching presents a variety of ways to kick-start idea generation.

Fashion is designed to be worn by people, yet people differ hugely in their tastes and spending power. Taking time to 'undress' the fashion market and identify its different sectors will help you to define who you are designing for. This is discussed in Chapter 3: Market Research.

Making the best use of the resources typically found in a library are explored in Chapter 4: Informational Research. The possibilities offered by shopping as a research activity are also explored. An array of hands-on approaches to primary research forms the basis of Chapter 5: Creative Research. Both two- and three-dimensional creative explorations are discussed at length.

Chapter 6: Fabric Research takes a close look at cloth. The goal of this chapter is to encourage a curiosity about fabric, and to build your knowledge of fibres, fabrics and their terminology. The impact of colour is demonstrated in Chapter 7: Colour Research. This provides a basic introduction to colour theory and explains the use of colour wheels. From these foundations you will be able to build up your knowledge and create colour palettes with confidence.

Chapter 8: Concept Development discusses what happens once you have completed your primary and secondary research activities. How do you make the most of your collated research? How do you interrogate your findings? How do you fine-tune your concept? These and many more questions are addressed. This chapter takes you through the design development procedure, ending with the preparation of finished sheets for your portfolio – the culmination of the research process.

You will find a true companion in *Fashion Design Research*. Numerous quotes from students and professional designers, combined with a wide variety of images, will inspire you at each stage of the fashion design process. ENJOY!

1.
What is Research?

As a fashion designer, research is part of your everyday life. Inspiration can come from anywhere, at any time. There are methods that you can use to spark ideas, which all designers use – primary and secondary research. But how much research should you do? How do you keep your search on the right track? This chapter will show you how to ensure your research has depth and relevance, which will, in turn, generate collections that are creative, innovative and unique.

What is Research?

Top
Fabric draped on a tailor's dummy.

Centre
Sketchbook showing primary research: experimentation with dyeing techniques and exploration through the modelling of fabric.

Bottom
Sketchbook showing the use of secondary research resources.

Research is fundamental to fashion design and provides the starting point for any collection. Without it there would be no design – or certainly no good design. Research can be conducted at any time and involves observing the world around you, and collecting and recording objects, images and ideas that inspire you. ***Primary research*** is new research, created by you; ***secondary research*** involves collecting material created by others, which you might find in books or on the internet, for example.

Your research can be part of an ongoing process, collecting day to day, or you can choose to research for a particular project or brief. It should not be perceived as an arduous task, but rather an opportunity to discover a treasure trove of potentially useful ideas.

10

Research is integral. A wise man once said to me, 'Fashion does not come from fashion', and it's so true.
Carolyn Massey

For me it is very important to absorb the world's cultures. These construct your particular way of communicating, and provide a way to go beyond your own 'mental home'.
Romeo Gigli

Research can take the form of mood boards, nights out or a trip away somewhere. It's a complete creative process where nothing is left out of the equation.
PPQ

The Value of Research

Fashion research is a creative investigation that can yield ideas, which then inspire and contribute to the design process. The deeper the investigation, the more design opportunities it will provide – thorough research allows more links between the layers of research material to be made, simply because there is more material to work with. Superficial research, as the name suggests, just skims the surface; fewer links can be made, so it usually results in design ideas that have undergone insufficient development. Research should define the concept and the creative direction through a process of assimilation and editing. By researching you are searching, or searching again.

The fashion industry by its very nature is ephemeral – it is fast-paced and subject to change over very short periods of time. Nothing in fashion is totally new; it is a cycle with reinvention at its core. The ability to innovate – to create the 'new' – is developed through strong research application, which is, therefore, an essential skill for a designer. Designers cannot create within a vacuum; they are like sponges, constantly absorbing the environment around them to find the inspiration needed to create a point of difference – 'newness'. Whether engaging with technological advances in fabric or reacting to a current political mood, designers are at the forefront of creative endeavours.

A cohesive collection results from strong research application where silhouette, proportion, line, fabric and colour are explored. In this collection, opaque felted fabric is paired with ultra-sheer chiffon, the blocks of colour divide the body in an interesting way, and the emphasis on the shoulders creates a top-heavy silhouette.

11

Primary Research

Top
Drawing at the 'Tommy Nutter: Rebel on the Row' exhibition, at the Fashion and Textile Museum, London.

Bottom
Drawings made at the 'Yohji Yamamoto' exhibition at the Victoria and Albert Museum, London.

Primary research is a first-hand investigation. It consists of material created by you that did not previously exist. A wide range of methods are used to gather and collate this, including experimenting with fabrics, taking your own photographs, making collages, and sketching indoors, outdoors, at galleries, museums and other places of interest.

When sketching at a gallery, you (the important ingredient) interpret an exhibit through drawing. Your focus should be on recording the elements of the exhibit that inspire you and can be of use. These can include anything from colour to form, texture and silhouette.

1992 S/S
crêpe de Chine

BLACK PLEATED
SKIRT IN HOMAGE
TO MADAME GRÈS
& WHITE SHIRT.
S/S '05
COTTON SILK

W99
Grey Tweed Jacket
& Skirt w/gathered
waist-
A/W 08-'09.
Wool.

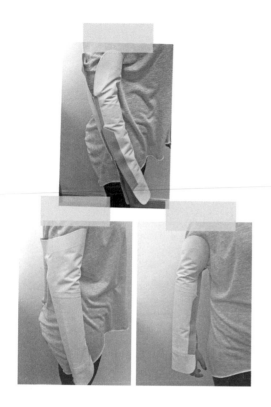

Creating fabric samples, experimenting with design details and manipulating fabric are very hands-on approaches to fashion research – for many designers these provide the starting point of a collection. Issey Miyake, for example, is renowned for his use of pleated fabric (see page 127), and fabric manipulation is central to his work. Working on a tailor's dummy also allows you to explore and research silhouette, proportion and form, enabling you to realize or interrogate your two-dimensional sketches and designs in three dimensions.

Top
Shirt sleeve samples made by bonding fabrics. This piece was inspired by a concept-led approach, exploring the utility wear of nurses in hospitals.

Bottom
Experimenting with projection to decide on the print of a jacket for a collection.

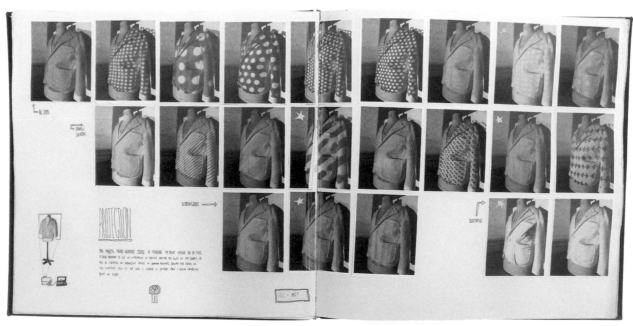

13

Top
*The fabric samples
on the right-hand
side have been
inspired by the
artwork images on
the left-hand side
of the sketchbook.*

Bottom
*Experimenting with
fabrics to further
explore your concept
can inform both how
you design and what
you design.*

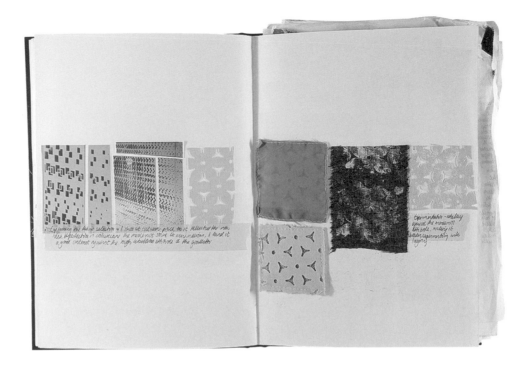

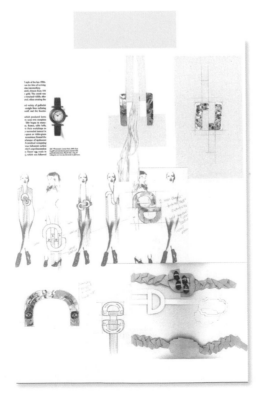

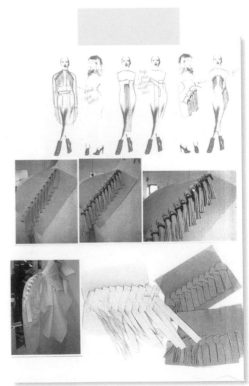

Photography also fits under the heading of primary research. This is frequently the quickest method of recording research material. You can use a camera to document inspirational objects and places. You can also photograph your experiments while ***modelling on the stand*** (tailor's dummy). This will provide you with images that can themselves prove inspirational. Photo-manipulation techniques, using software such as Photoshop, will then allow you to experiment with your images, which again can prove to be stimulating.

Top
Photography is a very accessible form of primary research. Dedicating a day or so to venturing out with your camera can be fun and rewarding, yielding numerous inspirational images.

Bottom
Working on a stand exploring ideas is a form of primary research. As you make adaptations, photograph each stage for future reference – for example, when working on design development.

Street style photography documents fashionably dressed people; it is a form of reportage that will give you an excellent opportunity for hands-on research. Many designers draw inspiration from the street. In turn the street can draw inspiration from the catwalks and, by the process of appropriation, transform it into something altogether new. Street style imagery is available everywhere, from magazines to books and online. The nature of the internet also makes images accessible and allows emergent trends on one side of the globe to influence street style on the other.

There are many street style bloggers who frequent markets, bars, clubs and the international Fashion Weeks in search of interesting-looking people. Knowing exactly where to go to maximize photographic efforts is key – it is important to have your finger on the pulse.

Creating a collage of found objects, images and other ephemera can be classed as primary research, too, because although the objects existed before, the collage did not. (Within art and design a 'found object' is one that was not originally intended as art; having being found, or 'chosen', however, it takes on an aesthetic value.) Collage as a primary research endeavour has many uses at various stages of the research and development process; see Chapter 5 for more information. Fundamentally, creating a collage provides a reasonably quick and spontaneous way to document ideas. The process of exploring and experimenting with different materials and images to create stimulating visuals can be fun as well as thought-provoking.

More information and ideas on how to undertake primary research can be found in Chapter 5.

ACTIVITY ACTIVITY ACTIVITY ACTIVITY

Invest in a camera that is portable and user-friendly. Over a period of a month, take a photograph every day of something you find interesting and inspirational. Only one image a day is permitted – be spontaneous. Once the month has ended, develop the images, display them in a book and review them.

The traditional Inuit clothing on the left has inspired the colours, textures and naive stitch details shown in the collage on the right of this sketchbook page.

Why Undertake Primary Research?

Why draw or take photographs when you can buy postcards, photocopy from books and download imagery from the internet? Why do you need to engage with the world at large when you can comfortably research from your workstation at home? The answer in a word is 'experience' – your own personal experience of the world around you is valid and worth exploring. There is a marked difference between reading a book or seeing a film and being told about that book or film by someone else. This is because first-hand engagement allows for your own interpretation of an experience, uncompromised by the views of others.

It is hard to beat the stimuli gained from first-hand engagement with objects and places. Touching, smelling, hearing and tasting are all very evocative experiences. There are numerous theories on how children learn and make sense of the world, but first-hand experience plays a major role. Touching a piece of fabric gives you an understanding of its properties – it might be cool to the touch, soft and supple, or thick and warm. Smells, sounds and tastes frequently evoke childhood memories or help to create links between past and present that can potentially inspire a whole collection. Seeing the true colour palette of a painting in a gallery, as opposed to its representation in a book, can often come as a big surprise. Reproductions of images are often poor impersonators; their colours can appear quite flat next to the rich hues of an original.

Research is the backbone of a collection. Not necessarily just visual research but also collecting and memorizing feelings, situations, emotions. This information goes through our system and becomes a more tangible theme. Research becomes less subconscious from this point.
Sachiko Okada – Blaak

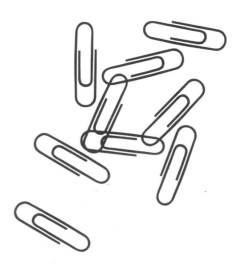

Secondary Research

Secondary research is research already in existence that has not been created by you. It helps to broaden the scope of any investigation by enabling you to access objects, places and facts that are not readily available to view first-hand. A wide range of research methods fall into this category. An activity as enjoyable and relaxing as flicking through a fashion magazine and tearing out pages of interest is sound secondary research. Reading around a subject, using search engines, and working your way through a mountain of books bookmarking pages to be photocopied are other methods.

Material can be gathered in the form of images and text from books, magazines, postcards, journals, videos, the internet and many other sources. The library is a very good place to start too, as they often house several different forms of secondary research material under the one roof.

Be aware of the varying quality of reproduced images. Photocopying or scanning images at 300 dots per inch (dpi) produces good-quality high-resolution images. A fair percentage of online images are of low resolution (often 72 dpi), which results in a pixelated image – this should be avoided at all costs.

Referencing historical objects and artefacts, such as period costumes, is another activity that you will frequently engage in. An awareness of past fashions is an essential part of fashion knowledge, so frequent exposure will enable you to establish good foundations. It might not always be possible to find a specific costume on display at a museum, but you might find it in a book or on a museum's website.

More information on how to access and use this wide array of resources can be found in Chapter 4.

Research is what defines each season or collection. It starts with the very first decision – to make a new collection – and, from that point on, everything that enters the arena plays a part as research. So, at that stage I try to surround myself with what I understand to be the 'right' stuff for the season, including good books, films and images.
6⁷/₈

A 300 dpi high-resolution image (top) and a 72 dpi low-resolution version of the same image (bottom).

Why Undertake Secondary Research?

The results of secondary research can be extremely useful and far-reaching. Whether you need to source historical imagery or enquire into the solar system, secondary research resources will often provide a far more accessible and immediate starting point than primary research. As a student, after receiving any project briefings from your design tutor, you will most likely find yourself in the university library to begin with, embarking on your initial research via secondary resources.

Top
Cuban woman smoking a large cigar.

Bottom left
Peruvian woman carrying a baby, Ollantaytambo.

Bottom right
Cupola of St Basil's Cathedral, Moscow.

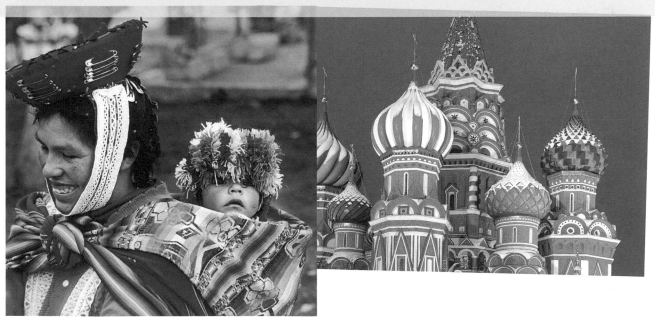

Allocating Time for Research

Toileing, sampling and three-dimensional experimentation are an important part of any design project and should be evident in some shape or form.

A designer's ability to innovate is heavily dependent on research that involves deep investigation. However, the length of time needed to research adequately depends on the timeframe of any given brief, or project. The timeframes given for briefs within a college can vary greatly from those in industry; often they are comparatively longer.

To make the most of your available time, it is worth planning in advance how much time you should give to research. To do this you will need to work backwards from the deadline, calculating how long the various stages of the design process (including sampling and making, if specified) will realistically take you. Everyone works in a different way; some need longer for the research stage, while others need more time for the making stage.

For a 10-week project, for example:

- Week 10 might be spent creating the finished sheets of designs for your portfolio, using computer-aided design or hand-rendering techniques.

- Weeks 9, 8, 7 and 6 might be spent on pattern cutting (making), and then making an outfit up in calico (muslin) or the real fabric.

- This takes us to the mid-point. Here you might allow two weeks (weeks 5 and 4) for documenting initial ideas and then moving on to design development.

- You might then decide that you can devote the first three weeks to initial research – collecting visual material, sketching, taking photographs, gathering fabrics, samples, haberdashery and fastenings, and so on.

The above-mentioned stages are not mutually exclusive, however – there is a tendency for some overlap. The length of a project will significantly affect how much time you allocate to research and the other stages of the design process.

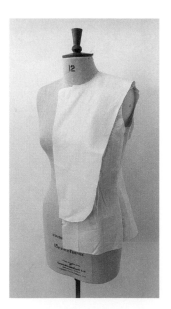

Keeping Research Relevant

While engaging in explorative research it is important to think about efficiency. What can you derive from the research in order to design clothes? Sometimes, when there is a lot of collected material, it can be quite difficult to see what is important – to identify the potential creative direction. This also applies when dealing with abstract material. Periodically throughout the research and development process ask yourself the following questions:

- Can I derive a silhouette from my research?

- Is there a suggestion of a colour palette that I can explore?

- Does my research point to certain fabrics?

- Can I derive details?

- Does the research allow for playing with proportion? If so, how?

- Have I made the most of any cultural influences?

- Have I explored references to detail sufficiently?

- Is there any suggestion of fabric manipulation that I can explore?

- Have I made the most of any historical references?

These will hopefully keep you on track by making your research relevant to the task at hand – that of designing clothes.

A collection based on an A-line silhouette developed through explorative research.

25

Silhouette

The silhouette is the overall outline of a garment or outfit. It is the first thing the eye sees before focusing on the details. A silhouette defines a collection through an emphasis on a specific element: for example, well-defined exaggerated shoulders and extremely low dropped-waist trousers (bumsters) were signature silhouettes explored in early Alexander McQueen collections. Historically, the dropped waistline epitomized the 1920s silhouette, as did the miniskirt, which was also instrumental to the short silhouette of the swinging 60s.

Proportion

Proportion in a garment or outfit is based on the silhouette. Proportion relates to how the body is divided into parts, and how the parts then relate to each other. The body can be divided vertically, horizontally or diagonally, and also in a range of other ways. Experimenting with the placement of blocks of colour or fabric help to emphasize proportion.

Line

The line of a garment is synonymous with the cut of the garment. Here, the focus is on the placement of seams and darts around the body and how they work visually. Typically, vertical lines work best to exaggerate the length of the body, while horizontal lines exaggerate the width of the body; curved lines tend to convey a sense of femininity, whereas straight lines are associated more with masculinity.

Cultural References

Looking at cultures in general – whether your own or those of others – can provide useful reference material to be applied to your research process. Cultural references can relate to dress, architecture and music – in fact, all manner of things.

Historical References

Period, as well as contemporary, costume (dress) provides a useful historical reference for fashion design research. Period costume can be found in specialist museums or illustrated in books, paintings, journals and online. Clothing has evolved quite dramatically over time – different eras have supported different emphases on the human form that have frequently reflected the trends of specific times.

Cultural and historical references will help you to explore different perspectives on silhouette, proportion and line.

Your Research is Unique to You

Research methods are unique and personal to every designer, and are reflected in their final designs. The Bless label – the product of two designers – is solely about a conceptual creative output. Situated between fashion and art, their products can range from clothing to an experience. Their conceptual (experience-driven) way of realizing garments pervades all facets of their work, including the shops they are sold in. The Berlin-based shop interior, seen here, reflects the anonymity of the design duo. Are you in a shop or an art gallery?

The individual designer heavily influences how research is collected and collated. In fact, their approach tends to mirror their personality – it might be haphazard and disorderly, or neat and uncluttered. The interpretation of the material, too, will be as unique as the designer themself. Even when working from the same body of research, interpretations will vary from individual to individual.

For uniqueness to materialize it is essential that the 'handprint' of a designer is evident in their research. This provides a point of difference and acts almost as a guarantee for a body of work that is less about imitation and more about creation.

It's the ugly things I notice more, because other people tend to ignore the ugly things.
Alexander McQueen

The research process is very important if it progresses naturally. In other words, it needs to be exciting and enjoyable. I do like the research process, especially when floating ideas start to become concrete design tools. It can be an idea, a thought, something that I might have started thinking a season before.
Bora Aksu

Research is an Ongoing Process

It is good practice always to be aware and on the lookout for inspiration. Make a habit of collecting imagery and found objects of interest, even when they seem irrelevant to your current project – they might prove useful in the future. Too often when looking for inspiration we tend to disregard things that displease us. However, if something has caused a reaction in you, even a negative one, it can still be worth keeping and investigating further.

Fashion designers operate within a cycle of two alternating seasons – Spring/Summer and Autumn/Winter. Each September–October and February–March, a different collection emerges from the depths of design studios located in New York, London, Milan or Paris. Some designers create two **cruisewear** collections as well, which brings the total up to four collections during the course of a year.

Within the timeframe of a season a lot of activity takes place. This includes going to international fabric fairs to order fabrics, designing, creating patterns, sampling, producing a collection, showing it at the international Fashion Weeks, selling the collection and manufacturing it. With all this activity the time available for research is less than expected, and there is never much time to procrastinate because the following season is always just around the corner. This is why it is important for designers to engage with the culture around them and beyond for inspiration at all times.

The S/S and A/W prêt-à-porter fashion year cycles.

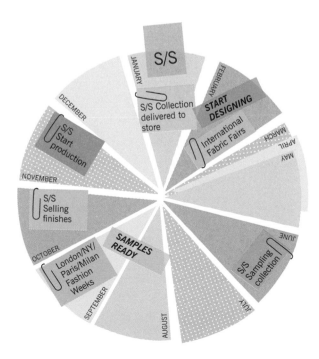

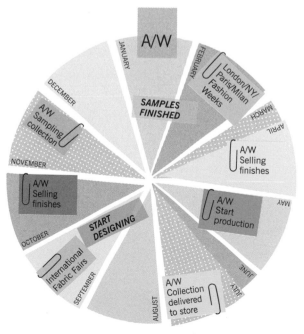

2.

How to Start Researching

Most design projects will start with some kind of a brief, even if it is just one you create yourself. This chapter will look at the different kinds of brief you will encounter, as well as some methods to get your research started, including brainstorming techniques and spider diagrams. Fashion design research is primarily visual research, so this chapter will also look at how to move from words to images, and how then to document that research effectively in a sketchbook.

What is a
Design Brief?

A selection of
university briefs,
which have been
written to inspire
and develop creative
thinking and problem-
solving abilities.

A *brief* signifies the inception of any project within the creative industries. Within a college a fashion design brief outlines the aims and objectives of a particular time-bound project, typically within specified parameters – a specific season, a genre (menswear or womenswear) or a brand, for example.

The duration of a project will vary; both short and longer projects have their merits and their difficulties. Shorter projects (from one to five weeks) help to improve your decision-making and application abilities, however good time management is essential for making efficient use of the allocated time. Longer projects (five weeks or more) allow time for more thorough research. These projects usually result in some form of construction, such as a *toile* (muslin) and/or garment. Good time management is also needed on a longer project, so that an adequate amount of time is spent on each of the different stages of research and development. Sustaining your interest and enthusiasm for a longer period can be quite a challenge, although re-engaging with your research periodically will help.

A member of the academic staff, or a visiting lecturer, will usually hand out written briefs at the start of a session in which they will also relay any other important information, such as the aims and objectives, timetable, the staff that will be working on the project, hand-in details and more. A briefing session will also give you the opportunity to ask questions and to discuss any elements of the brief that you feel need clarification.

A brief is designed to inspire active engagement with a project. It will offer a variety of problem-solving opportunities as you work through all the stages of the research and development process towards the final outcome. This will allow you to question your aesthetics – building upon or disregarding them – as well as your design integrity, and may frequently take you out of your comfort zone. All of these things are necessary if you are to create designs that are unique, fresh and new, time after time.

Different Types of Briefs

As a student you will encounter different types of briefs serving different purposes. The aims and objectives will differ, as will the outcomes and assessment criteria. Some projects will have to be presented to the rest of your student group, others you will just hand in on the day of submission. This multifaceted experience is designed to enhance your teamwork abilities, brand and market awareness, self-motivation, time management, research skills, communication and presentation skills. There are five different types of briefs that you will typically experience as a student: the individual, the team-led, the collaborative, the sponsored and the competition brief.

You can apply a different approach to all of these briefs. You might, for example, decide to tackle a brief through market-led research, or through an emerging concept, theme or narrative derived from your research, or maybe through your inspirational muse (see Chapter 3). If it is not stipulated in the brief you can decide which method is best.

All briefs have the same purpose: they are designed to inspire and provide the momentum for idea generation. However briefs rarely offer you carte blanche; there are normally parameters of some kind to work within – either academic or external requirements. An academic design brief stipulates:

- The aims of the brief

- The learning outcomes – what you should learn as a result

- The assessment requirements – what you need to complete and submit by the end of the project

- The assessment criteria – the guidelines by which your work will be assessed.

The aims stipulated by a brief will relate back to the programme of study being undertaken. An 'Introduction to Design' brief, for example, might aim to:

- Introduce you to the processes of research, development and design

- Enable you to explore the integral relationship between the two-dimensional image and corresponding three-dimensional form

- Introduce the basics of pattern cutting, manufacture and sample room practice

- Enable you to develop professional illustrative and presentation skills.

Learning outcomes relate back to the aims and stipulate demonstrable learning. For example, by completing the brief you will learn how to:

- Generate and explore ideas

- Demonstrate how to develop and apply illustrative and presentational methods and techniques to the resolution of ideas

- Demonstrate basic techniques of garment construction.

The Individual Brief

Typically set by a member of staff or a visiting lecturer, an individual brief will demonstrate how well you work on your own. You should therefore always make sure you understand what is being asked of you from the beginning; ask for clarification from your tutor if you are unsure. Good time management is an essential skill for fashion design, and engaging in this type of brief will flag up areas for personal improvement. You might, for example, find that more time spent on research in greater depth will benefit you in the long run. You might also find you need to improve in other areas, such as presentation skills. An individual brief provides an opportunity for your personal aesthetics to shine through, while also displaying your capacity for problem-solving.

The Team-led Brief

How well do you work with other people? Do you like to lead? Are you happy being told what to do? What do you do if someone in a team is not pulling their weight? How often do you need to meet to brainstorm? Have you taken on too much? Have team members been designated equitable amounts of work? Who will co-ordinate everybody's efforts? How are you managing your time? Who will present the work? A team-led brief allows you to experience the simulated reality of a fashion design team or, on a larger scale, interactions between the different faces of the fashion industry – textile designers, photographers, PR (public relations), fashion stylists and more, depending on the specifics of the brief. In these situations many of the above questions are a consideration.

Individual roles within a team are typically designated by the group members themselves. Team-led briefs by their very nature tend to be challenging; group dynamics have to be managed while the team works to create a successful product. The individuals brought together to work as a team may or may not know each other. However, it is always important for the group to gel. A poorly led team, or one where there is infighting, is unlikely to produce a good design.

The Collaborative Brief

A collaborative brief involves co-operation between a minimum of two distinct but interested parties. This can typically be the pairing of two or more students from the same discipline or from two or more different disciplines. A typical collaboration in industry is where a professional designer joins forces with another designer, label or brand.

The premise of a collaborative brief is that two minds are greater than one. It can be pretty challenging working on an even playing field with another person or company. The rewards, however, can be great, and new solutions to old problems will often arise.

BURBERRY

The Sponsored Brief

Universities continually make efforts to form links with industry to enhance the student experience. The employment of visiting lecturers, who typically work in industry as freelancers or in a full-time capacity, demonstrates this to a degree. The sponsored brief is another example.

Typically, a sponsored brief will be set by a textile mill or a fashion company, although it may sometimes come from a company from a completely different discipline. The prizes offered for such a brief can range from anything from a work placement to a cash incentive. Both academic staff and a representative from the sponsoring company will assess your work, either during a presentation or when work is submitted.

The Competition Brief

A competition brief tends to engage a wider community of students. It is normally set on a national scale by a company that values an association with emerging talent. Work placements, cash incentives and travel bursaries are typical of the prizes awarded to the winners, while the company benefits from the boost to their profile.

Inspiration

What is inspiration? It is a word that is used with great frequency in the creative industries, and is considered an essential element of any artistic endeavour. Inspiration can be defined as a mental stimulus that enables you to do or feel something that is creative in nature. On a spiritual level, inspiration can also be defined as a divine influence that immediately engulfs the mind or soul. Without inspiration, both creativity and innovation would cease to exist.

As designers we need inspiration to create the proverbial 'fire in the belly' – it not only kick-starts any project but also provides the momentum to work through all the stages of the design process. So, do the same things inspire us all? At times yes, but more often than not different things inspire different people. Discover your own stimuli and build upon them by engaging in diverse experiences.

Inspiration is a magnificent thing. It's difficult to explain where it comes from; it is something given to you. If I were religious, I'd say it comes from up above.
Ann Demeulemeester

I need many things to nourish my inspiration: objects, images, stories and pieces of cloth. Anything that can make my mind travel and work. I continuously need to see new things, new places, to meet new people to listen to. At the same time, I need to be sure I can still count on old, steady things – things with a past and that have already belonged to someone else. Things that have outlived time.
Antonio Marras for Kenzo

Vintage issues of Vogue *are very inspiring, particularly for looking at the contemporaries of the better-known designers of certain periods who didn't receive the same recognition. There are so many cutting techniques and details to be found that may not have been fully explored, and it is exciting to use them in modern garments.*
**Chris Brooke –
Basso & Brooke**

Fabric is my starting point. I'm known predominantly for colour, prints and embroidery – normally the more they clash, the more I like it. Fabrics give me my initial inspiration and represent, for the most part, the essence of what my collections look like.
Dries Van Noten

I always like there to be a bit of a story to each collection, and I always have this idea of the muse, so I am always thinking about that.
Peter Jensen

I love reading biographies and I love real life. I often feel that real life is much more fantastical than anything that comes from our imaginations. Real life is much more interesting than anything you could dream up.
Christopher Bailey

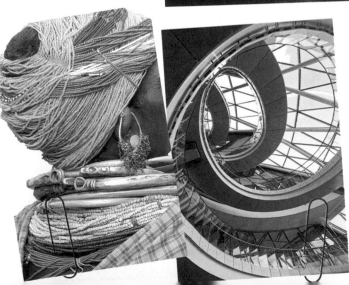

LIFE! I think the education imparted to us gives us a culture that is ours, upon which we base ourselves, and from which we take our inspiration. This inspiration evolves along with the evolution of our background.
Martin Margiela

How Do I Start Researching?

After a briefing it is not unusual to feel a bout of excitement, anxiety or even a mixture of the two. You might be fortunate enough to have several ideas running through your mind during and after a briefing; at other times you may be quite perplexed as to what and how to research. In either case, having a methodology to get you going will prepare you to make the best use of your time. Taking notes, brainstorming and creating spider diagrams are accessible and effective ways to unlock ideas. All you need to get started is a pen and a piece of paper.

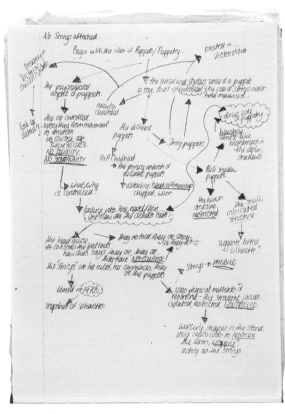

Note-taking

A briefing and lecture provide the perfect environment for note-taking, as do technical demonstrations in the sample room given by a sewing technician or pattern cutter. You do not necessarily need a separate notebook; making notes on the handouts provided by your instructors ensures that you are more likely to re-read what you have written. If you do choose to use a notebook, though, select one that is compact. The habit of note-taking has many benefits:

- It helps to increase your attention span

- It allows you to retain information that you have read or heard

- Note-taking during a briefing will help you formulate questions that you might need to ask for further clarification of the brief

- Rephrasing text in your own words can aid a better understanding of the task

- Highlighting key words or sentences that appear problematic will maintain your focus.

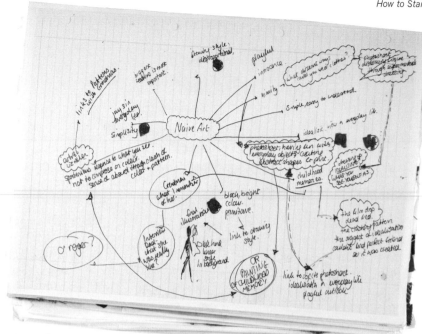

A spider diagram exploring the possibilities for research based on the term 'Naive Art'.

Brainstorming

A **brainstorm** is an effective problem-solving tool that can be used both individually and also within a group to generate creative solutions or ideas in response to a brief. Designating an adequate length of time to this soon after a briefing is highly recommended.

Typically, a group brainstorm involves all the participants shouting out ideas, which are then noted down by one person on a large piece of paper. The diverse experiences of the group members can provide a wealth of different ideas. Participation from all the group members is encouraged – a positive environment is created if everyone feels that their ideas are of value. Initial, unformulated and, at times, 'out there' ideas can be tailored into viable yet unconventional ideas that solve problems creatively.

If you are brainstorming on your own, write down ideas as they come to you on a large piece of paper. You can then maximize the usefulness of this pool of initial ideas using spider diagrams.

Spider Diagrams

A **spider diagram** (or, sometimes, mind map), is generated from one main idea, which is written in the middle of a piece of paper and represents the spider's abdomen. Further ideas are then drawn off the main idea as if they were the legs of the spider. This cycle is repeated, with these new ideas becoming the main ideas of their own mini-spider diagrams and generating further ideas, and so on.

Spider diagrams generate ideas with relative ease and produce remarkably effective results. The belief is that they mirror the way the brain works – unlike linear notes – by starting with a central idea that then branches out, generating an infinite number of different possibilities. They also allow you to explore visually the relationship between words on the page, opening up your immediate area of research and adding depth to your investigation.

... And What Else?

Sometimes the best way to start working on a brief is to engage in some form of escapism. Distracting yourself from the task at hand, whether by going for a long walk, visiting an exhibition or going to a vintage fair, will allow your brain to wander freely – it might be just the kick start you need. Become that proverbial sponge and soak in all that you encounter. Have a loose timeframe for escapist activities in mind, and then return to your project, hopefully with renewed vigour (if not a new approach), ready to embark on research.

Choose a word from the following selection: security, grey, eclipse, structure, uniform, red, nature, danger, kaleidoscopic, constriction, circus, Victoriana.

STEP 1
Create a text-based spider diagram. Think connotations, symbolism, representation, word association.

STEP 2
Find relevant imagery.

STEP 3
Create an image-based spider diagram that represents the text-based version.

How to Expand Your Research

Spider diagrams and brainstorming generate ideas in the form of words on paper. However, words alone do not suffice in fashion design research; they need to be fully explored and substantiated using imagery and/or objects. Both primary research endeavours (photography, drawing or painting, for example) and secondary research (such as taking photocopies from books, magazines and journals) will help you to explore different perspectives. Try to be imaginative – this will lead to the broadest possible spectrum of possibilities.

There are many different ways to expand your research, each one personal to the individual. However, the college environment will give you the opportunity to learn about different methodologies, and to expand and diversify your methods. Assessment presentations also provide an excellent opportunity to observe how other students approach this stage. Be inspired – perhaps try something different with your next project.

Choosing a subject to base my project on, is for me, the most difficult part. I'll begin by creating a mind map, exploring the different areas that a subject could lead me towards. The subject has to be something that I am interested in for me to feel motivated. Once I've chosen a subject I will read up on it – visiting the library and using the internet to give my research an intellectual base. I also visit relevant places, such as exhibitions and stores, to gather my research. **Hefina Williams**

My research always starts with a lot of reading. I then visualize the theories/stories I have found by searching through magazines, books or relevant art exhibitions for material to help describe my main idea.
Danya Sjadzali

I generally look at things that I genuinely like aesthetically. Usually it will start with just one image that I have seen or found, and I will build up a range of images that work together with that one to form some kind of mood or general look.
April Schmitz

I tend to start researching via history books and people-watching. I like pitching up a stand somewhere in central London and watching all the people of the city go about their business. **Alice Overington**

How to Document the Process – Sketchbooks

What is the best way to document and collate all your research findings?

A sketchbook is the format chosen by most designers from across the creative disciplines. This provides a space where the design process – from initial thoughts to final outcomes – is documented and developed. In addition, any ideas not used to answer the current brief can be kept and may provide a starting point for future work.

A sketchbook should contain *triangulation* between primary and secondary research resources, annotations, colour palette development, *fabric story* development, initial design ideas and design development (if you choose not to use a layout pad – see Chapter 8). Triangulation is best described as the manifestation of initial design ideas through the links made between various research sources. Good triangulation occurs when an initial design idea brings together various elements to produce a total effect that is greater than the sum of its parts.

A sketchbook also allows you to integrate both secondary and primary research materials. Secondary resources used by themselves have the tendency to de-personalize research and make it appear flat and one-dimensional. It is good practice, therefore, to create links between secondary and primary imagery in your sketchbook, positioning them side by side, disparate alongside like-for-like imagery. This visual cross-over, will inspire yet more links and, thus, new design possibilities.

Sketchbooks come in many shapes and sizes, so make sure you choose one that is appropriate for your needs. Tips for selecting the right sketchbook can be found in Chapter 5.

Form Follows Function

Top
The links made through collected research material has resulted in this line-up of six outfits.

Bottom
Sketchbooks provide a 2D format for documenting your ideas via a process of experimentation and exploration. A working sketchbook demonstrates a process trail, in which development is evident.

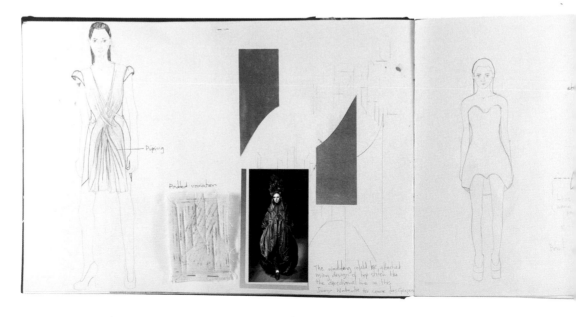

Top
A combination of
primary research
(in the form of
notes and a fabric
swatch) and
secondary
research (in the
form of imagery) has
inspired this sketch
of a man's jacket.

Bottom
Hand-rendered
imagery is given
context by supporting
secondary imagery.

Opposite page:
Top
These three
secondary research
images have elicited
a response that is
evident in the initial
design ideas. The
silhouette of over-
sized and layered
garments shows in
the sketches, as do
the woolly hat and
baseball cap. These
initial ideas will then
be developed and
refined further in
the research and
development stage.

Bottom
This page acts as a
mood board within
the sketchbook,
creating a narrative.
It successfully
demonstrates the
concept, the colour
palette under
consideration and the
fabrics to be used to
make the collection.
A lot of thought has
been put into the
composition and
layout of this page.

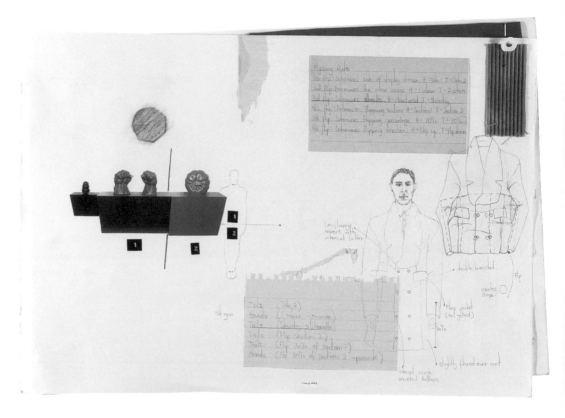

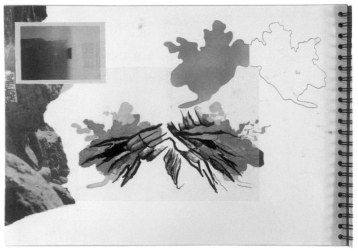

44

Starting a
Sketchbook

Top
*Starting a new
project often
entails starting a
new sketchbook.
The first page in a
blank sketchbook
can be particularly
daunting. If it proves
too challenging,
simply try turning
the page over.*

Centre
*The methodology
employed here
involves working on
single sheets with
the intention of
compiling a bound
sketchbook in the
later stages of
the project.*

Bottom
*The different
elements on this
double-page spread
– fabric samples,
3D experimentation
on a tailor's dummy,
secondary research
imagery, annotations
and initial design
ideas – demonstrate
a good level of enquiry
and exploration. A
strong process trail
is evident when
exploration and
experimentation
continue across
several pages of
a sketchbook.*

Starting a new sketchbook can be both exciting and extremely daunting, but various techniques can be used to alleviate any anxiety. These can range from skipping the first page to working on single sheets with the intention of compiling the sheets into a book later. There are no hard or fast rules – however, it is always best to leave perfectionism at the front door. The sketchbook is a place to work through ideas, not a finished piece of work.

As you gather material, creating different layers, annotating, experimenting and exploring, your sketchbook will become more engaging for you and any potential viewer. It is paramount that, just like a diary, it reflects your own personal processes. This is what will make it distinct and relevant to your particular project. There are also a number of strategies you can use to achieve good triangulation in your sketchbook, including cross-referencing and juxtaposition.

Cross-Referencing

Different sources will normally have different perspectives on any given subject/ object, and relying on a single source can render research one-dimensional. So the practice of cross-referencing – comparing material from different sources – is necessary for both validating and enriching your ideas. This applies to both textual information and visuals. Multiple sources will help to enhance your understanding and research possibilities by providing different levels of information too – some more detailed than others. For example, you might be interested in Victorian Gothic architecture; to develop a good knowledge of this subject, relying on one image will not suffice. A broad selection of imagery, offering a range of similarities and differences, will be much more informative.

Imagery relating to the homeless has been sourced from various books, and from different photographers with different perspectives and aesthetics. Drawing on mutliple sources builds up a more thorough knowledge of a subject.

Juxtaposition

A nineteenth-century waistcoat is juxtaposed with a graphic image using negative and positive space, an image of a wooden sculpture and a piece of corrugated tubing. By considering elements of the waistcoat design, ideas have been conceived and explored.

Trying to unleash the potential in your research is your first and foremost goal. There is often a tendency to keep all the individual strands of your research separate. This can happen as a consequence of sticking research imagery into a sketchbook too soon, thereby creating 'chapters', with a lot of starting and stopping.

To create an organic flow, begin by simply collecting any imagery – do not stick any of it into your sketchbook immediately. Look through what you have gathered and play with *juxtaposition*, which is the placement of (often contrasting) images alongside each other. The greater the contrast between the images, the greater the juxtaposition. Alternatively, when sticking down individual strands of research, leave space for other strands of research to be stuck down alongside them later. Always leave space for initial design ideas too. This approach will create links between disparate imagery, and expand your design possibilities.

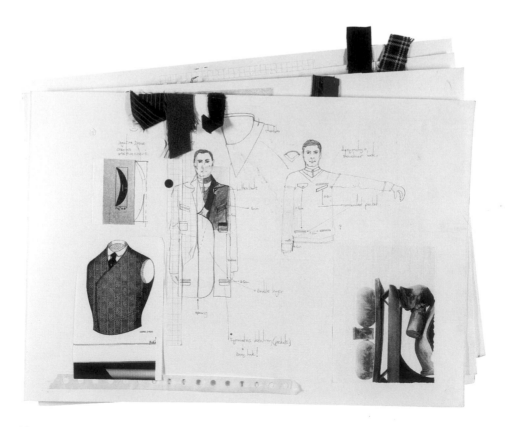

Top
Exploring the notion of symmetry within the abstract, various areas have been cross-referenced here – reflection in water, the intricate design of butterfly wings, splodges of paint that create a mirror image and a catwalk image from the Iris van Herpen Spring/Summer 2010 collection.

Bottom
The secondary research imagery in this double-page spread has elicited a response. Fabric suggestions, as well as initial design ideas influenced by the silhouette evident in the images, have been included. Links have been created and consequently triangulation is evident.

Scrapbooks

Magazines provide a healthy source for tear sheets. Referencing a variety of magazines for inspiration is good practice, as different publications will have their own editorial style. Backdated issues are also an invaluble resource, and collections of these are often held by libraries.

A scrapbook is a place in which predominantly secondary research resources are gathered – magazine tear sheets, newspaper clippings and photocopies, for example. A scrapbook will contain little or no evidence of any primary research endeavours, so, unlike a sketchbook, will be devoid of any design process or input from the designer.

A scrapbook simply provides a useful place to store things of interest for future use – a reference source – and will consist mainly of things created by other people. It has the potential to continually grow and become vast.

1980s NEW ROMANTIC

PRINCE

THE EARLEY EIGHTIES WAS THE ERA OF THE NEW ROMANTICS, INSPIRED BY THE FLAMBOYANT PERIOD COSTUME AND VIVIENNE WESTWOOD'S 'PIRATE' COLLECTION. THE STYLE OF DRESS WAS SWASHBUCKLING WITH GILT BUTTONS, GOLD TRIMMINGS AND FLOUNCED SLEEVES. PIRATE ESQUE BOOTS WERE WORN WITH TROUSERS TUCKED IN AND OFTEN A SASH WAS WORN AROUND THE WAIST SIMILAR TO PIRATE COSTUME.

MICHAEL JACKSON'S THRILLER VIDEO HUGELY INFLUENCED MENSWEAR. OVERSIZED, SLOUCH SHOULDERED LEATHER JACKETS WITH MILITARY OR HISTORICAL ACCENTS WERE WORN BY TEENAGERS AND POPSTARS. THE COMBINATION OF RED AND BLACK, SIMILARLY TO THE THRILLER VIDEO ALSO BECAME POPULAR. JOHN PAUL GAULTIER COMBINED RED AND BLACK FOR THE FILMS SET AND COSTUME DESIGN. TROUSERS TUCKED INTO HEELED BOOTS, AS WORN BY SPICA WERE INFLUENCED BY THE PIRATE LOOK ESTABLISHED BY VIVIENNE WESTWOOD.

MONEY LUXURY

THE RICH, TRADITIONAL COLOUR SCHEME OF THE DINING AREA IS ENHANCED BY THE PERIOD INFLUENCES AND OSTENTACIOUS INTERIOR DECOR, FOR EXAMPLE THE FLOOR LENGTH CURTAINS, DRAPES AND TASSELS.

THE CINEMATOGRAPHY IS VERY CLEVER BECAUSE, DESPITE THE CHARACTERS APPEARING TO BE WEARING THE SAME OR SIMILAR COSTUMES - THEY CHANGE COLOUR AND COINSIDE WITH THE COLOUR OF THE SET - THEREFORE EACH 'ROOM' OF THE RESTAURANT HAS A CERTAIN MOOD', DUE TO THE CONTINUITY.

Top
Scrapbooks tend to have very little evidence of primary research. This example shows three superimposed secondary research images. The text, though hand-written, has been copied from a book or magazine.

Bottom
None of the secondary images in the scrapbook have elicited any type of personal response.

51

CASE STUDY

DOMINIC LOUIS

Louis Mairone grew up in the greater Philadelphia area, in the US, where he studied fashion design at high school. Relocation to the Big Apple became inevitable once he made the decision to follow his passions in this field. He attended the Fashion Institute of Technology for further training, graduating with an associate's degree in menswear. This was followed by employment at design house DDCLAB, as an assistant designer, but it was not long before Mairone established his own label – Dominic Louis, in 2010.

Mairone's designs are influenced by his love of New York City – its urban landscape, people and everyday happenings. Soaking up all the androgynous subcultures that surround him results in versatile unisex collections that push the boundaries of identity. 'I'm very inspired by what is happening in my life at the moment. Whether it's from meeting with another artist, the news, or just the perfect moment … I think my current reality really shapes where my artistic mind seems to go. I think as artists we subconsciously incorporate all of that into our work. I try and meet it head-on, wholeheartedly, and incorporate it into the work season after season. I want to look back ten years from now and be able to tell the definitive story of Dominic Louis.'

Mairone describes inspiration as 'an extension of our initial brand identity and how we have grown and learned over the past season. We only get to live each moment in our lives once. My inspirations are very reflective of that, and also what will progress the collection, move it forward. In the process, we're listening to our clients, supporters and contributors. Inspiration is all subject to that – the moment when all of these conversations collide and you and others feel something new emerge; something you've never felt before.'

Developing concepts for different collections 'starts with an idea, and turns into a mood board. A lot of times the ideas are spread out. This is a way to bring them all together. We add and take away things from the board over the span of a few weeks. As we try new styles, those that work can be placed on the board to be built upon. Our clients are constantly moulding us by what they react to. They are very influential when it comes to our board.'

The Dominic Louis label marries a futuristic fashion-forward aesthetic with exquisite handcrafted techniques that show an attention to detail. Fabrics are often luxurious and exotic – previous collections have been made from cashmere, fox fur, alpaca, raw silk, buffed croc and leather. Marione's menswear tailoring roots add to this juxtaposition further, with the introduction of masculine lines, shapes and cuts to the womenswear line. There is often a post-apocalyptic, utilitarian and edgy undertone to his collections. Mairone says, 'Our work is raw, like the end of the world, where the skills of generations of couturiers have been absorbed and adapted to fit the needs of the average city nomad.'

3.

Market
Research

Engaging in market research creates an awareness and understanding of the different levels of the fashion market. It is vital that you have a sense of the end-user for your designs – the consumer – to keep your work relevant. This chapter explores the fashion market and shows how you can visualize your customer, either by using a muse or by looking at brand identity, advertising and trend forecasting to gain an insight into who they might be.

Researching the Market

Opposite page:
Top
Y-3 store in
Conduit Street,
London. The
Y-3 collection is
a collaboration
between Yohji
Yamamoto
and Adidas.

Bottom
Topshop store in
Oxford Circus,
London.

To understand the different levels of the fashion market, close inspection is needed. Whether you find yourself in a shopping mall, high street or department store, there are distinguishing features to note. The question 'Which market are you designing for?' is a crucial one, and frequently crops up during the stages of a project. In fact, the answer to this question should be known at the start of any project. This will allow you to take a closer look at the market and establish which areas you find interesting. You might find you gravitate towards denim, sportswear, eveningwear or conceptual design. You may find that you are drawn particularly to the designer level of the fashion market, or you may discover that the high street engages you more.

Just as there are different types of designers, there are different levels within the fashion market to accommodate them. Where will you fit within this ever-expanding market? The following considerations are largely influenced by the level of the fashion market you are designing for: How much can you spend per metre or per foot for a chosen fabric? How many seams can a garment have without increasing the cost price significantly? How broad a range of sizes is necessary? How many pieces do you need to have in your collection?

On a wider scale, a closer inspection of the market will also enable you to gain an understanding of competitors and their share of the market, the market size, and the consumer and emergent trends. The collection, analysis, reviewing and interpretation of data – data that has been collated through research of primary or secondary resources, or a combination of the two – best supports this understanding. In market research, primary research typically involves collecting original data using the following methods:

- Interviews
- Questionnaires
- Focus groups
- Surveys.

Secondary research frequently involves collecting data that already exists, using sources such as:

- Books
- Trade journals
- The internet
- Magazines.

The collated primary and secondary data will fall into the category of either quantitative or qualitative research, or both. Quantitative research, as the name suggests, is focused on quantity: for example, a survey conducted with a large sample of respondents will result in quantitative data. It typically provides information on consumers and on market share.

Qualitative research relates to quality – providing data that explains the 'how' and 'why' of the market. It is a lot more organic in approach and in the types of data collected; it is very useful in giving an insight into how consumers think and feel about a wide variety of issues. Face-to-face interviews, for example, will give qualitative data.

Fundamentally, fashion falls into two distinct groups, covered by the French terms **haute couture** and **prêt-à-porter**. The first translates as 'high fashion' – the most fashionable and influential dressmaking and design. The second translates as 'ready to wear'. Haute couture is a thin slice of the market. The majority of fashion seen, bought and worn by the average consumer is prêt-à-porter. The following breakdown of the different market segments will help clarify the differences between these, and the levels that exist in between.

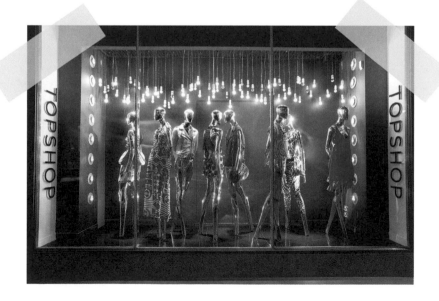

Haute Couture

Haute couture is an extravagant and costly business to be in – no expense is spared. The clothes are specific to an individual customer, just like the principle of a tailor-made suit. The fabrics are the finest and the garments employ the handcrafting skills of the most able seamstresses. Making garments is frequently very time consuming and can take months of dedication and patience. The industry supports the very finest specialist makers in fashion, from embroiderers to weavers and beyond. Permission to use the 'haute couture' label (backed up by French law) is restricted to just a handful of fashion houses, who meet with the strict requirements of the Chambre Syndicale de la Haute Couture.

To qualify, a fashion house must:

1. Offer more than one fitting per order; each order is always for an individual private client

2. Have a studio based in Paris with at least 15 full-time employees

3. Employ 20 technicians in their studio

4. Show twice a year at the Paris couture shows.

Today, though, there are fewer haute couture houses in Paris than in the heyday of the 1940s and 50s – and far fewer clients able to afford this type of luxury.

Haute couture shows are biannual, taking place in January and July, just ahead of the prêt-à-porter Fashion Weeks. They provide great advertising for their brands, showcasing lavish lifestyles. They also represent the pinnacle of unrestricted creativity.

Prêt-à-porter

Fashion that does not satisfy the specifications of haute couture, or is not made for an individual by other bespoke methods, is by default prêt-à-porter, or ready-to-wear fashion. Prêt-à-porter is mass-produced and, therefore, much cheaper to purchase. It comprises a range of standardized sizes for the buying public, the fabrics used tend to be more affordable, and the number of hand-worked techniques are greatly reduced.

Ready-to-wear fashion covers a wide range of varying products, from fairly exclusive *super-brands* to cheap and cheerful supermarket brands. Designer ready-to-wear collections are shown at least twice a year in the fashion capitals of New York, London, Milan and Paris (and some designers also create two cruisewear collections a year). However, new fashion capitals are also emerging, which aim to show their own country's ready-to-wear collections, such as Stockholm, Berlin, Rio de Janeiro, Amsterdam, Bangalore and Madrid.

Though designer ready to wear is more ubiquitous than haute couture it is still of very good quality, exhibiting great craftsmanship, innovation and exclusivity; it is also pricey. Designers such as Erdem, Anne Valérie Hash, Etro, Anna Sui and Antonio Berardi, and super-brands such as Louis Vuitton, Moët Hennessey (LVMH) and Gucci, all create ready-to-wear collections.

The lower end of the ready-to-wear market – the high street and the supermarkets – are influenced by the designer catwalk collections and consequently create watered-down versions for their own lines. High street labels such as Topshop, H&M, Mango and Whistles are very trend-orientated, and are very quick off the mark in designing and producing lines that can appear on the shop floor within weeks. Supermarkets are much slower to cover current trends.

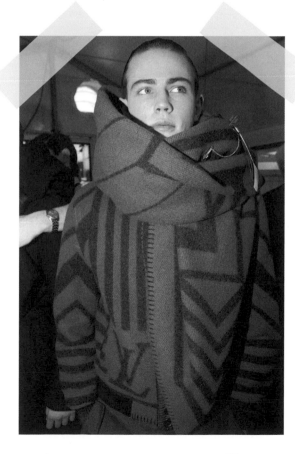

Louis Vuitton prêt-à-porter menswear, Autumn/Winter 2012.

Luxury Super-brands

LVMH and the Gucci Group are both prêt-à-porter fashion conglomerates and are positioned in the market as luxury super-brands. Under the ownership of the LVMH group are Louis Vuitton, Loewe, Celine, Givenchy, Marc Jacobs, Fendi, Donna Karan, Emilio Pucci, TAG Heuer, De Beers and many more. The Gucci Group owns Alexander McQueen, Yves Saint Laurent, Stella McCartney, Bottega Veneta, Balenciaga, Gucci and Boucheron. Luxury super-brands have huge budgets to spend on advertising which promotes a luxury lifestyle with all the trappings.

Mid-level Brands and Designers

Mid-level brands and designers are a lot smaller and consequently less powerful than the super-brands. Nevertheless, they are household names in their respective countries and some are also recognized at an international level. Mid-level designers show at the various Fashion Weeks, where buyers seek out collections. Both mid-level designers and brands are sold in department stores, independent boutiques, franchises, and in their own stores, if they have them.

Collaborative ventures between mid-level designers and high street stores are gaining in popularity. Well-known designers Jasper Conran and Julien Macdonald have designed lines exclusively for Debenhams department store – 'J' and 'Star by Julien Macdonald' respectively. H&M has also witnessed a flurry of designer collaborations, with Maison Martin Margiela, Karl Lagerfeld, Stella McCartney, Comme des Garçons, Viktor & Rolf, Roberto Cavalli, Marimekko, Marni, Matthew Williamson and Sonia Rykiel. These collaborations ensure exposure for the designer, and prestige for the store – and make designer labels accessible to the average person on the street.

Independent Designer Labels

Independent designer labels operate on a much smaller scale than the mid-level designers. These designers – who work with a team to help realize a collection – often own their own label. The team will normally consist of a freelance pattern cutter (maker) and seamstress. Independent designers will often wear several hats at the same time – while trying to manage aspects of the business such as cash flow, sales and press relations, they will also have to find the mental space for designing a collection.

Trade fairs are a popular choice for independent designers, and some might even manage to secure finance or sponsorship in order to show at a Fashion Week, where there is the chance that their collection may be bought wholesale to be sold at boutiques and department stores.

Casualwear and Sportswear Brands

Nike and Levi Strauss are two of several well-known super-brands in casualwear and sportswear. They are very influential and make their presence known using good advertising that helps keep their brands within the public eye. The fact that both labels are so ubiquitous is proof of their success – you are never too far from either brand.

There are also a few mid-level brands and designers within the area of casualwear and sportswear: Evisu, Diesel, Hugo Boss, G-Star, Stone Island, Armani Jeans, Dolce & Gabbana and Replay are a few examples.

High Street

High street fashion is the category of the market offered by chain stores, which means that a particular shop can be found in different cities all over the country, and sometimes globally, too; H&M, Topshop and Zara operate on an international scale. High street brands create or buy in different collections within a season to meet the majority of their consumers' needs – suits, jeans, swimwear, accessories, etc. These collections have been directly influenced by trends identified at the prêt-à-porter Fashion Weeks.

The time taken to produce a collection from drawing board to shop floor (lead time) is a fraction of that required by a mid-level designer to create a ready-to-wear collection – weeks instead of months. And because production involves large quantities, manufacturing for the high street is given priority by factories.

The fabrics, cut and attention to detail can sometimes be compromised in this area of the market. However, the ability to be on-trend quickly, coupled with reasonable price points, broadens the consumer demographic considerably – everyone is interested in what is considered a comparative bargain.

Supermarkets

Clothing lines are rapidly gaining ground in an environment once restricted to food and household goods – consumers have started to buy into this level of the market due to its affordability and improvements in design. Prices are kept low because of the large quantities being manufactured quickly. In the UK, 'George at Asda', 'TU' by Sainsbury's and 'Florence & Fred' by Tesco are all private-label goods that have a strong position within this market. 'George at Asda' is stocked in around 500 stores in the UK. Asda itself is owned by the American supermarket giant Walmart, and Walmart also sells affordable fashionable clothing lines (including 'George') in its US stores, while in France, hypermarket Carrefour stocks similarly priced ranges.

Competition

There is fierce competition in the market place – all retailers bid for sales from the consumer, at times the very same consumer. Identifying and analysing the competition is invaluable for effective market research. To assess the competition, four key factors have to be considered:

- The positioning of the brand or product within the market place
- The type of product or brand and its purpose
- The psychology of the consumer
- The variety of shopping environments.

The interplay of these factors (some fixed and others variable) creates the competition that is evident in the market place.

Analysing the strengths and weakness of competitors is essential in helping you assess how best to compete. This analysis will enable you to evaluate a number of things, for example the performance and operation of competitors – their resources, their share of the market (market share), the size of their operation, the services on offer and much more. Trade and industry published figures also provide an insight into and data on these points.

Billboard advertising the David Beckham bodywear range at H&M. Celebrity endorsements and collaborative ventures are great advertising tools that help in a competitive market place.

The Muse

When designers put pencil to paper to sketch a design idea, in the majority of cases they have someone in mind who will wear it, even if it is initially themselves. This someone can be an individual – a muse – or they can represent a particular group of consumers (a *demographic*). Who is this person? This question provides a good starting point, and as your research and development skills mature, your answer to it will become more defined.

A working definition of a *muse* is a goddess, or the power, that inspires a poet, artist, thinker, or anyone working in the creative industries. The concept of a goddess muse might seem slightly outdated, but it is all too evident that certain individuals – both historical and contemporary – inspire designers to create collections.

Examples of muses include both men and women – Anna Piaggi, Agyness Deyn, Jackie Onassis, David Bowie, Sienna Miller, Grace Jones, James Dean, Katharine Hepburn, Charlize Theron, Catherine Deneuve, the Duchess of Cambridge and Marlene Dietrich, to name a few. What they have in common is a strong sense of style and the ability to project a particular lifestyle. The overall package then provides a benchmark for a designer's ideas. A muse can also be real or imagined. Frequently, an imagined muse is a concoction of characteristics from several real people, and can be just as potent as a real individual.

However, the role of a muse is not necessarily a passive one. Muses may often act as a sounding board for designers during the design process. The late Isabella Blow was friend, muse and mentor to the late Alexander McQueen. Lady Amanda Harlech, one-time muse to John Galliano, is currently muse and creative assistant to Karl Lagerfeld; she works as a pair of second eyes for him on the Chanel, Fendi and Karl Lagerfeld labels, as well as appearing in promotional material. A muse can generate a lot of PR for a designer by helping to promote and establish brand identity on many levels.

I don't really sit down at the beginning of each season and try and figure out who this elusive muse is. But at some point in the creative process I go through a series of questions in my head. Is this for someone who exists today? Is there someone I can think of who would wear something like this? I think that process makes me believe that something is credible or has a reason to be. I like to know that there is someone I can think of who would like to wear whatever it is I am designing.
Marc Jacobs

I tried to throw myself into imaging that glamorous jet-set world of the Gucci woman, though it was a long way from my own life.
Christopher Bailey

Brand identity

The fashion market is saturated by brands that range from haute couture houses to the affordable clothing lines of supermarket chains. It is therefore crucial for any brand to establish a clear identity to distinguish itself from others – a ***brand identity***. A brand can be a name, design, symbol, a unique feature and so much more. Consumers have a tendency to buy into brand names – a positive perception of a brand can relate directly to an increase in sales figures – so brand identity is something to be nurtured and protected. If a brand is perceived positively, consumers will return time and time again. A clear brand identity indicates that a business is effectively answering the needs of their target market on a regular basis.

Brands are omnipresent – from Marks & Spencer to Ralph Lauren, Etro, Celine and Louis Vuitton, you are never more than five minutes away from one. Some brands, due to their presence in high-end fashion magazines and exclusive shopping districts, frequent lavish billboard campaigns, high price points and perceived exclusivity, are desired by the masses but affordable only to a few. The Louis Vuitton brand falls into this group. Other brands market themselves on their affordability and accessibility by advertising in mid-range fashion magazines and selling via their own chain store outlets – River Island and the Gap are examples of these. Whatever the level, good advertising and PR help to keep a brand in the public eye.

In a design project you might be asked to design for a brand – you might even be asked to create a fashion brand of your own – so you need to understand how brand identity works. You will need to identify the consumer demographic you are targeting. Whom do you want to buy your brand? What is their lifestyle? Do they have a disposable income? Are they male or female? Ask yourself these and other similar questions so that your brand is relevant to your chosen consumer. You can learn how to answer many of these questions by looking at how other brands position themselves in the market.

Demographics

Demographics provide statistics on a given aspect of the human population – gender, race, income, age, stage in life, lifestyle and much, much more. Demographics create segmentation of society at large, creating smaller groups (sub-groups) with a commonality. These sub-groups are easier for the retailer to understand and subsequently target. This is a widely used method of classification.

Humorous Uniqlo cashmere advertising campaign pitching to a demographic that enjoys luxury fabrics at affordable prices.

Advertising

Advertising has a huge impact on consumers' perception of a brand. By studying the advertising of an individual brand you can not only identify their particular style, but also their position in the market. For example, brands that can afford to place substantial advertisements in high-end magazines are normally at the higher end of the market. Dissecting and analysing advertising provides a sound area of research when trying to make a better sense of the relationship between brands and consumers.

Within fashion, advertising can take place in many forms. Retailers, such as H&M, Benetton, Harrods and American Apparel, often use billboards, having reasonably sized budgets for large campaigns. Retailers also use their shop fronts as an advertising tool. Mid-level designers, if they have the budget, advertise in fashion magazines – magazine spreads provide great advertising and publicity and are free, although a fee must be paid to the PR agency that is overseeing the brand and loaning items to fashion stylists and editors.

Public Relations

In unpacking and researching brand identity it is good to be aware of the presence and influence of good PR. As well as advertising, good PR helps to give a brand a public platform. A PR agency is employed by the designer or brand to represent them and to get publicity. The level of representation varies depending on the fee paid. Essentially, PR agencies build good relationships with stylists, editors, journalists and writers so that the designers or brands they promote are represented in the media.

PR agencies organize and oversee promotional events, including catwalk shows. They send out gifts to revered editors and aspirational celebrities. They also compile press releases, which are sent out to key editors and others working in the media. Following up on releases is an important part of the job. Feedback on the publicity generated is then passed on to the designer or brand.

Top
An assortment of fashion catwalk show tickets. These are distributed to key people within the fashion industry by PR agencies.

Bottom
Screen shot of the Fashion Monitor – a comprehensive directory of contacts, news and events in the fashion, lifestyle and beauty industries.

Trend Forecasting Agencies

Promostyl trend board.

To understand the fashion market it is important to understand the importance of *trends*. What makes an item of clothing fashionable one minute and not the next? Why do hemlines change? Why is green the new black? Where do trends emerge? What are macro and micro trends? Who uses them? Who provides them? Imagining a trend as something emerging from the bottom of a funnel is a neat way of understanding how a trend has usually evolved from something much larger. Trends emerge from the societal issues that penetrate all walks of life, from the way we think to the way we live.

A *trend forecasting agency* joins up the dots. Information from diverse sources is gathered and broken down, and the common ground is investigated to assess how it relates to fashion. These diverse sources include blogs, journals, theatre, film, books, newspapers and the internet, amongst others.

Trend forecasters must be constantly aware of current thinking and culture (the zeitgeist), whether that is keeping abreast of celebrity lifestyles or changing consumer attitudes.

Promostyl, Worth Global Style Network (WGSN) and the Future Laboratory are prominent trend forecasting agencies. Promostyl create **trend books** and trend boards that anticipate emergent trends, focusing on aspects such as silhouette, colours and fabrics. WGSN provides fashion intelligence to the industry through an online presence, by following street fashion, looking for trends in arts and culture, keeping up with pop culture, referencing vintage and other similar activities. The Future Laboratory uses **ethnographic research** tools such as interviews and surveys to provide its clients with fashion intelligence.

High street fashion companies tend to use trend forecasting agencies to assist with designing collections. Luxury super-brands, mid-level designers and brands, and independent designers, on the other hand, tend to generate their own personal vision of a trend. As a student you will also generally be required to rely on your own personal analysis of emergent trends, rather than relying on the forecasts of a trend agency. Engaging in the research methods that the trend agencies themselves use – following street fashion and engaging in arts and culture, then using a process of assimilation, dissection, editing and analysis – is good practice. Being aware of the influence of macro and micro trends will also increase your understanding of the subject.

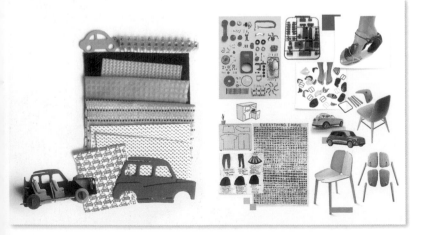

Macro Trends

A ***macro trend*** is the result of a large-scale societal change. For example, the world's population is ageing, and this change in consumer demographics has huge implications for fashion and other industries. What is becoming clear is that older people are becoming more style conscious. Since they have cash at their disposal, new markets might emerge as a result. A lack of awareness when it comes to significant societal upheavals like this can be a very costly mistake for any business.

Micro Trends

The term ***micro trend*** was coined by Mark Penn, a strategist and adviser to such prominent individuals and companies as Tony Blair, Bill Clinton, Bill Gates, BP and Microsoft. Micro trends are smaller trends established by small groups of passionate people who run counter to the mainstream – they can affect societal change, shaping tomorrow. A group may consist of just 1 per cent of the total population, yet in a country the size of the US this will mean a group of about 3 million people, highly capable of making a significant impact. Young knitters, social geeks, caffeine crazies, surgery lovers, sun haters, vegan children and the uptown tattooed are all examples.

Young knitters, to take one of these examples, are on the increase in the US, inspired by A-list celebrity enthusiasts such as Cameron Diaz, Julia Roberts and Sarah Jessica Parker. The interests of these crafters run counter to the high-tech, technology-driven environment they occupy. As this group is composed predominantly of young women it is highly probable that craft outlets will begin to stock goods aimed at a younger clientele. Catwalk shows will also probably include more handknits in the future. The young knitters are part of a 'nesting' trend, too – a 'do it yourself' wave, evidenced in the increase of cookery, house-buying and house-renovation programmes on television. This trend is also reflected in the customization options now offered by some household names: Nike and Timberland have both produced sneakers that come with a range of stickers, glitter glue, stamps and graffiti markers.

Top
Fashion and Textiles graduate collection, shown on older models.

Bottom
Hand knitting is gaining popularity amongst a younger age group. More and more people are knitting their own garments or accessories.

Ethical Concerns

***Sustainable fashion*, or eco fashion, is a rapidly growing micro trend within the fashion market.** Familiar stores such as Marks & Spencer now offer some items in organic cotton or wool, while People Tree, a fair-trade pioneer, has a concession at Topshop. Sustainable fashion aims to adhere to environmental and social responsibilities, and carbon footprinting, cotton production, sweatshops and child labour are some of the key concerns.

A ***carbon footprint*** is the total amount of carbon dioxide produced by the processes needed to produce an item, including its manufacture and transportation. Carbon footprinting can therefore be used in fashion to measure the environmental impact of producing a particular garment. Sustainable fashion aims to reduce carbon footprints by, for example, transporting materials and finished products over shorter distances, thus cutting fuel emissions considerably.

Cotton production involves the use of heavy pesticides, which has devastating effects on both cotton producers and the environment. Several of the chemicals used are highly toxic, and World Health Organization figures suggest that in excess of 20,000 farmers lose their lives every year. It is argued that if cotton farmers were paid more for their goods, they would be able to diversify their produce and use more environmentally friendly farming methods.

Organic cotton is produced without synthetic pesticides and fertilizers. As a consequence, both the cotton farmer and the environment benefit greatly. Farming methods such as crop rotation also greatly reduce pest numbers and increase numbers of natural predators. Although garments made from organic cotton are usually more expensive than those made from regular cotton, more and more retailers are stocking organic cotton to meet growing demand for it.

Sweatshops are factories found in developing countries, where working conditions are unsavory, wages are poor and the rights and wellbeing of the workers are overlooked. High street brands are often accused of perpetuating their existence by insisting on short delivery times and keeping prices low (low prices depend on low wages in sweatshops). However, other levels of the fashion market have also been known to use sweatshops.

Child labour is prevalent in most developing countries. Impoverished large families send their children out to work to earn money for the family. Children are employed in factories because they are cheaper to employ, enabling factory owners to earn larger profits and ensuring cheap prices for consumers. In many cases, however, these children work in hazardous conditions for very long hours, making this a key issue for brands wanting to offer a sustainable product.

CASE STUDY

DILYS WILLIAMS

Dilys Williams, director of the Centre for Sustainable Fashion at the London College of Fashion (LCF), merges her talents as a fashion designer, innovator and leader effortlessly. Williams is a passionate spokeswoman for sustainable design, and actively promotes it within the academic sphere and beyond. She is also responsible for Fashion and the Environment, a groundbreaking master's degree designed to affect change in the fashion industry at grassroots level, primarily through external collaborative ventures.

Sustainability within fashion is slowly gaining momentum, but redressing the balance requires a major shift in attitudes, as Williams acknowledges. 'So much is changing – I do feel that the huge increase in our connections makes us more aware of our interdependencies, more at ease with diversity, more active as citizens – but there is also a huge dumbing down of realities due to the short termism of most governments and businesses. But I remain optimistic – as long as we never think that we've nailed it, as long as we keep on moving in the right directions.'

Preconceived ideas about sustainable fashion mean that a concerted effort must be made to ensure that it is marketed and perceived positively. 'The challenge is in moving from this current business model to others that can continue to achieve that novelty, engage people in meaningful employment and be able to adapt to the changes in the ecosystem and the economic system, by imagining better ways to achieve our human needs for identity, connection and belonging.'

The Shared Talent initiative partners local craftspeople from different parts of South and West Africa and India with LCF students in research projects that draw on the wide-ranging experiences and knowledge base of all involved. These collaborations centre on considered design, and work as a catalyst, facilitating change within communities.

Williams' design background at both designer and high street level provided her with first-hand experience of the decisions that can be made to address sustainability – for example, prioritizing organic materials and sustainable production methods where possible. Designing for Katharine Hamnett (also a pioneering eco-activist), in particular, brought a new level of awareness of ethical and ecological issues and how to marry them with desirable, uncontrived design. As Williams reflects, 'I have always aimed to contribute relevant design work and have always had a curiosity around what fashion is, does and stands for – so to remain relevant, I seek out what is happening in the world. Having said that, it was really when I started to design for Katharine Hamnett that many realities started to unfold, and since then I haven't looked back. New ideas continue to flow.'

Today Williams uses a broad range of media – television, journals, newspapers, radio and magazines – to bring attention to and promote the ecological issues within fashion. Her philosophy hinges on the belief that by engaging with the ingenuity of others as well as your own, you can help to craft a world that we can all be proud of.

ACTIVITY

Compare and contrast the little black dress in two different market levels. Compare cost, fabric content, cut and fit (take photos). For further analysis, write up a customer profile based on your own experience of the respective shopping environments.

Left
Zoe Fletcher actively engaged with each element of the knitwear process, from shearing sheep, developing dyes, spinning, designing and knitting the collection, to show British fashion contextualized in its time and place.

Top right
Una Hussey's collection maximizes heat retention through materials that warm and embrace the body, responding to ecological and economic necessities and the need for creative solutions to the problems of resource depletion, energy costs and climate change.

Bottom right
Exploring empathy, sustainable and behavioural economics, and the psychology of affection, this jacket by Ivan Dauritz narrates a story of its making and offers spaces for the wearer to continue the narrative in its layers.

4.

Informational Research

Visual research is an integral part of fashion design – the concept, theme or narrative of a collection is often derived from inspirational imagery. Visual research is strongest, however, when supported by an in-depth understanding of its context. Luckily, when inspired by something, you will want to know everything about it! Allowing time to read around a subject – to engage in informational research (a form of research that gives you access to information) using secondary research techniques, as shown in this chapter – will enhance both your research prowess and your designs.

Libraries

Your college library is a great place to start when seeking informational research. Libraries offer a comprehensive visual and information resource, with access to a large database of printed and electronic books, exhibition catalogues, and printed and electronic journals via links on the library's website. There may also be access to a number of databases from outside the college, although these might be limited or require a password for logging on.

A multimedia facility is also a common feature and it provides an invaluable resource; many titles covering a wide range of genres exist in either DVD or video format. Most libraries provide viewing facilities with the use of headphones.

Extending your search to other libraries, whether college or public, can really intensify your search and boost your findings. You can often check the catalogues of other libraries online. It might also be possible to arrange an inter-library loan – check with your librarian. (There is usually a procedure to follow when enquiring about borrowing material from large public libraries – for example, the British Library in London requires you to fill in an online form.) It is highly unlikely that you will be able to borrow books from a college library that is not connected in some way with your own. However, photocopying (where there are no copyright infringements) and note-taking are usually permitted.

Finding Your Way Around a Library

Libraries can use different cataloguing systems, and these are often country-specific. For example, the Library of Congress cataloguing system is favoured by many US libraries, while libraries in the UK use the Dewey Decimal system. These and other systems provide easy navigation through the dense collections held within a library.

It is important that you become familiar with both the numeric system used by your library, as well as its general organization. Find out where the over-sized books and DVDs are stored, and enquire about access to backdated issues of magazines and journals. Find out how to operate the photocopier, and establish whether there is any limit on photocopying. Is there a scanner? How many books can you borrow at any one time? Are there any copyright issues that you should be aware of?

Most colleges offer a tour of the library at the start of the academic year, which is the perfect opportunity to gain an overview and ask any questions. In fact, one of the most invaluable resources to be found in a library is the team of librarians. They know their stock inside out, and typically have specialist knowledge.

Making the Most
of a Library

Spending random days familiarizing yourself with your library's resources will improve your research skills. Broadening your scope of focus within a library is also vital – variety in all its guises is key. There can be a tendency to find yourself in the same corner of the library, musing over the same pile of books and magazines. Experiment, explore, move about and read books and magazines on subjects that are unfamiliar to you. To broaden your knowledge and lay yourself open to the occasional eureka moment, you must broaden your scope and use the library's resources to their fullest. Simply leafing through piles of books and magazines left by other students can create an accessible bridge to the unfamiliar.

To make your visit to your library a comfortable and fruitful one, ensure that you:

- Eat and drink beforehand, as libraries prohibit food and drink on their premises

- Have a pen and paper to hand so that you can jot down any reference numbers from your catalogue searches. Torn paper also provides improvised bookmarks.

- Take your sketchbook – this is where you will eventually collate your findings

- Take your spider diagram – this will help with any keyword searches

- Take basic, dry art materials with you, such pencils and dry colour media

- Have a photocopier card, or the right change for the machine

- Take a memory stick and/or laptop

- Do not forget your library card.

Libraries are a key resource for informational research. Familiarizing yourself with the floor plan of your campus library will save you time in the long run.

Books

Dedicate some of your time to exploring non-fashion books catalogued in your campus library – pick books from shelves at random.

The potential for visual and textual inspiration from books is limitless. Depending on how large your college is, and the breadth of study courses offered, your library will house a comprehensive catalogue of subject-specific books, so it should be possible to avoid focusing purely on fashion-related books. Literally pick out random books from the shelves and have a flick through. You may just stumble upon something that is relevant to your current project – or a forthcoming one. Thinking outside the box during the early stages of research will greatly enhance your research and development process.

Collect Your Own Books

Why not start your own collection of inspirational books, covering your interests in fashion and beyond? Books are an investment but they need not cost the earth. There are many stores selling second-hand books.

There are also various websites dedicated to the recycling of books – Strand bookstore, AbeBooks, Gumtree and Amazon are good places to start. To keep things affordable, avoid first editions and out-of-print books where possible. Libraries also occasionally have clearouts, so you may be able to pick up a bargain there. Creating your own library will nourish and inspire you, and provide a conducive working environment at home.

Reading Around Your Subject

To influence the future, a good working knowledge of both the present and the past is vital. History is present in every aspect of life – everything has a historical underpinning, everything has a past. There are several renowned designers whose signature style is blatantly immersed in historical references; Vivienne Westwood and John Galliano are good examples.

You are not born with this knowledge; it has to be learnt. Looking at the catalogues of fashion and costume-history books in the library will start you off. Silhouette, proportion, fabrics, embellishments, use of colour, tailoring and more have changed significantly since the early days of clothing.

You must also make a habit of exploring the cultural issues of the contemporary world in order to contextualize your visuals. Cultural influences can come from distant, exotic lands, or can be found in your familiar everyday surroundings – both sources can be relevant, and may inspire creativity in all aspects of your work, from colour to proportion, fabric and more.

Magazines

Fashion magazines offer a great source of informational research, for both current and past fashions. It is important to note that **lead times** (in the production and print schedule) of approximately three to four months apply to monthly magazines. Fashion spreads in newspapers and their respective magazines have shorter lead times and so tend to be more current.

The numerous fashion magazines available range from mainstream titles such as British, American and Italian *Vogue*, *Elle* and *Marie Claire*, to the more edgy publications, like *POP*, *Lula*, *Wonderland* and *AnOther Magazine*. The latter often take more risks than mainstream titles, and tend to work with emerging and influential photographers, fashion designers, stylists and journalists.

All magazines have their own signature style, and any time spent on dissecting this will add greatly to your fashion knowledge and awareness of the market. Some questions to get you started in your analysis are: Which demographic is this magazine pitched to? Does it represent you? Do you aspire to it? What type of fashion does it represent – high street, designer or both? Is it mainstream or edgy? Is there a lot of advertising? Which brands are advertised? What is the distribution?

By looking through the designer collections featured in magazines on a regular basis you will get a feel for current trends – for example, what designers are using in terms of colour palettes, fabrics, silhouettes and proportion. Avoid the temptation, though, to borrow significant aspects of designer collections and pass them off as your own. It is crucial that your own unique inspiration provides the springboard for your work. Remember, too, to ask whether your library keeps backdated issues of magazines. These will often provide additional inspiration.

Contemporary magazines help you to keep up to date with current fashion and lifestyle, whereas backdated issues acquaint you with fashions past.

The Internet

The internet provides a window on the world. It can make the inaccessible accessible. It can save you a huge amount of time. However, it is also very easy to waste a lot of time when browsing online. Making effective use of this resource, therefore, is key to effective time management. How do you retain your focus? How do you manage your time online effectively? How do you check the accuracy of your results?

The internet can be a good way to gain access quickly to initial information for research purposes. However, it is important to be mindful of internet usage – becoming over-reliant on this resource can result in lacklustre design projects. The quality and reliability of imagery and information online should not always be taken at face value. Fashion design research does not start and stop in front of a computer screen – do not miss the opportunity to truly engage with other research methods and deepen the development of your concept.

Using Keywords

Effective use of keywords is crucial when researching online – being selective will make your research faster and more focused, whether searching on the internet or looking through a database. A spider diagram, or mind map, that you have created previously can often be a great source of keywords,

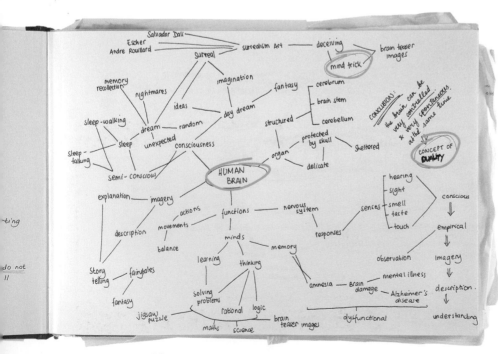

since these will relate directly to your project. To be more efficient:

- Make a list of keywords
- Investigate these words further – are there other, similar, words (synonyms)?
- Is there relevant terminology to be investigated? Look in a dictionary, thesaurus or encyclopedia for ideas. This itself can be done online.
- Make a checklist, marking items off as you move down it.

For example, your inspiration might come from the colour green.

- The keywords derived from green could be: nature, ecology, armed forces, geography, decay, recycling, forestry
- Possible synonyms: essence, conservation, army, cartography, decomposition, salvage, forestation
- Potentially relevant terminology: ontology, bionomics, the military, mortification, physical geography, regeneration, arboriculture.

From a single word ('green') 21 new keywords or phrases have been created. These new keywords will then form the basis of a focused, efficient online search.

Checking the Accuracy of Search Results

Search engines, such as Google, catalogue the infinite information found online through the use of a keyword or keywords. Searches frequently yield hits that might run into the thousands. So, a lot of results, but are they all relevant? More importantly, how accurate are they? Fact, fiction and opinion can be found in surprisingly equal measures on the internet. Other forms of media have quite rigorous systems at work to check for accuracy and authenticity. Books are edited, journals and papers are peer-reviewed; there is also a level of accountability in printed media. The internet is not controlled in the same way.

Always cross-reference any material you find online with information from other sites and offline sources. For example, Wikipedia frequently headlines the list of hits from a keyword search. Wikipedia is an online encyclopedia which any member of the public can contribute to and edit. While it can provide a starting point – a quick nugget of information – it always pays to check its accuracy against other sources. It is a useful tool, but make sure you use it wisely.

Use a search engine such as Google to research online using keywords generated by your spider diagrams.

Finding Images
on the Internet

A Google search can provide you with
a vast database of imagery. However, the
results of your search will be only as good
as the keywords you use. A fair amount
of imagery you find this way will also be
of low resolution.

Images can also be sourced from image
databases, which are catalogued and curated,
giving the feeling of flicking through the pages
of a book. These databases are typically
commercial, educational or image-sharing
sites. They offer a rich and diverse source of
visual imagery at the touch of a button.

Commercial databases normally require
registration and payment of a fee for image
usage. Usage rights will vary from one
database to another, and from image to
image – always check what is permissable.
Photographic Youth Music Culture Archive

(PYMCA), Alamy, Getty Images, Rex
Features, Shutterstock and Corbis all offer
comprehensive databases. You can access
imagery online or phone in to speak to an
in-house librarian.

Educational database sites offer the
download of high-resolution images for free,
solely for educational purposes. Examples are
Bridgeman Education, ARTstor and VADS.
Free images for educational purposes can also
be found in the image collections of numerous
galleries, libraries and museums. Terms
and conditions of usage will vary, so always
check. The Victoria and Albert Museum has
a good collection of historical images. The
British Museum, the Guggenheim and MoMA
also offer broad image databases.

Image-sharing websites such as Instagram,
Flickr, ImageShack and Photobucket offer
free images. However, this does not mean
that *intellectual property* rights have been
forgone. Through a globally recognized
Creative Commons licence, the owners/
creators can share their work and also define
the rights of usage – anything from no rights
reserved to all rights reserved, and everything
in between.

Online Magazines, Blogs and Social Media Sites

Most notable fashion magazines have a presence online, facilitating universal accessibility – something that is simply out of the reach of the corresponding hard copy. This presence makes it possible to see the latest from the Paris catwalks anywhere in the world, keeping everyone abreast of contemporary fashion.

Fashion blogs are a significant player on the web and provide current information on fashion and lifestyle. Blogs – from 'web logs' – came into existence at the start of the new millennium. They are basically online diaries that are shared with interested parties. Huge inroads have been made by fashion bloggers over the years, often at the expense of legitimate fashion journalists; some well-established bloggers have a larger readership and more influence.

Fashion blogs can be created by individuals and also by companies. There is a proliferation of these online, so it is wise to have some system in place to flag up the most popular ones – Bloglovin' or a similar aggregator does this effectively. Some of the top individual blogs are:

Cupcakes and Cashmere
cupcakesandcashmere.com

Jak and Jil
jakandjil.com

Face Hunter
facehunter.blogspot.co.uk

A Cup of Jo
joannagoddard.blogspot.co.uk

Twitter, Instagram and Flickr are good examples of social networking sites that can also provide current information about fashion, so are worth keeping an eye on.

Dazed Digital, the website of Dazed & Confused *magazine, explores the latest trends in fashion, music, art and culture, and photography.*

Copyright

When downloading images from the internet for your research, be aware that copyright applies to all visual work. In fashion photographs featuring models, the models themselves are protected by copyright, along with the photographer and the designer of the garments.

While researching, you will spend a reasonable amount of time finding, collecting and collating secondary research resources, whether textual or visual. Understanding how *copyright* issues might affect this process is important. Copyright legislation offers you and others protection of your intellectual property (your creative work, which is classed as an asset), safeguarding against the misuse of this asset in a globalized world. (This does not include an idea in the form of a thought, just work that has a physical presence.) The broad aim of the legislation is to ensure that no one uses a piece of work created by someone else, passing it off as their own. It covers text, images, films, and music and sound recordings – anything created, whether in physical or digital form.

You need to be aware of and protect the copyright in your own works and be aware of the copyright of others. Being knowledgeable about possible infringements from the outset is not so easy – legislation often varies from country to country, so there is no one international set of rules. Be aware of this variability and follow the laws in your country. Technology has also moved on with such speed that copyright legislation has failed to keep pace, leaving a great deal of uncertainty about the dos and don'ts of the digital image in particular. There have been no test cases to date to use as a benchmark.

Written permission for the use of written or visual work protected under copyright is required at all times, with the exception of work that is in use in 'the public domain' and work covered by 'fair use'. Work that is in the public domain is typically work with expired copyright. Work covered by fair use refers to excerpts of copyrighted work being used for study (non-profit educational purposes), criticism or comment. Always reference your sources; this is discussed in the next section.

Organizing Your Research

Spending ages searching through any research material is not the best use of your time, so try to establish a filing system and stick to it. There are lots of ways of organizing your material. The most important thing is that you choose a system that works for you, and that you will actually use.

You might have two systems in tandem – one for physical material and another for web searches, books, journals and the like. Box files, plastic wallets, expandable manila folders and scrapbooks are good for housing the former. Card indexing, using the Harvard system of referencing, and creating bookmarks on your web browser, using reference management systems like Delicious, RefWorks, Xmarks or Zotero, are all efficient methods for organizing the latter. You might also decide to categorize your searches further into groups under headers such as project name, artist, designer, colour reference or concept.

When using secondary research resources it is good practice to record and reference your sources. For example, when photocopying an image from a book, make a note of the photographer, the year the photograph was taken, the title of the image and also the title of the book. The same practice applies to images from magazines. This information will be very useful if you need to find the material again – whether it is to ascertain the context or seek out other images by the same photographer. In some cases, especially when using text, it also helps you guard yourself against accusations of plagiarism.

The information that is typically used in citing sources, whether for recording or retrieval purposes, is as follows:

- Book title
- Author/editor of the book
- Publication date
- Publisher
- Website address
- Date and time of search
- Name of artist
- Name of photographer
- Date of photograph.

I use everything from film and books to music and photography. I keep folders of things that may not be useful for another couple of years.
Emma Cook

Film

Cinema has a universal and far-reaching appeal, part of which can be attributed to the fashion seen onscreen. Film can inspire fashion, and vice versa; the two are related both aesthetically and commercially.

There are numerous garments that have made it from the big screen to the international fashion catwalks. The 1930s wardrobe of *Bonnie and Clyde* (1967) is believed to have influenced the renaissance of the beret and cardigan at the time of its release. After Tom Cruise was seen sporting retro aviator shades in *Top Gun* (1987) these shades were back in vogue. More recently,

Avatar (2009) inspired Jean Paul Gaultier's Spring/Summer 2010 couture collection, while Sofia Coppola's *Marie Antoinette* (2006) inspired Marc Jacob's Autumn/Winter 2012 ready-to-wear collection.

Both fashion and film are visual mediums that rely on a narrative, which is why the two can work so effectively together. The use of costume in film can, amongst other things:

- Convey an era
- Establish a character
- Create a spectacle
- Create an ambience.

Actively engaging with films, both past and present, will greatly enhance your secondary research possibilities. A film can inspire a colour palette, or a principal character might set the tone for a collection's narrative or theme – the possibilities are endless. Repeat viewing is recommended; it provides the opportunity to focus on the different aspects of a film, allowing you time to decode, analyse and gather the relevant information.

Choose an iconic film from any genre – one you find inspirational. Explore the film for useful research information and create a sketchbook. Consider the following in your analysis:

- *The historical context*
- *The cultural/social context*
- *The historical/contemporary details*
- *Can you derive a colour palette?*
- *What types of fabrics have been used?*

Museums

The Victoria and Albert Museum, London.

Museums are a rich resource for informational research. Besides providing an opportunity to draw (see Chapter 5), museums are designed to be multilayered and interactive learning environments that cater to a wide-ranging demographic. Museum collections are an obvious source of inspiration; however, museums also employ staff who are specialists in their field (appointments often have to be made to see a specialist) and can provide dynamic and enthusiastic information on their area of expertise. Museums often host lecture series, conferences and symposia that relate to temporary exhibitions as well as the permanent collections; sponsor artist-in-residence programmes; and provide access to online catalogues, libraries and study rooms, and to the museum archives (where this applies, it is by appointment only).

Some museums are dedicated to the history of fashion, or have a department with this focus. In London the Fashion and Textile Museum and the Victoria and Albert Museum (V&A), in New York the Museum at the Fashion Institute of Technology (FIT), and in Paris the Musée des Arts Décoratifs are invaluable sources for historical reference.

Left
*A 1922 Callot
evening dress,
petticoat and belt
on display at the
V&A, London.*

Right
*Detail of lace on a
gown from 1903–5.*

Shopping

Top
Evening shot of the world-renowned London department store Harrods.

Centre
Parade of boutique shops on Monmouth Street, Seven Dials, London.

Bottom
Study labels to investigate the different fabrics that are used in garments. Labels are normally sewn into the side seam of a garment, or underneath the brand/designer label at the centre back.

Opposite page:
Top
A vintage stand at the Pitti Filati fashion industry trade fair, Florence, Italy. Vintage accessories – bags, shoes and belts – are a good source of inspiration.

Bottom
Clerkenwell Vintage Fashion Fair in London is a great place to find unique items that can inspire a whole collection.

How can you gather informational research from shopping? As a fashion designer, invaluable contemporary and historical fashion information is gleaned from contact with garments. You are unable to touch a garment in a magazine, whereas handling a garment in person will allow you to identify its fabric type, observe the weight and fall of the cloth, see the details and scrutinize the fit.

Shopping does not always mean parting with hard-earned cash. 'Shopping around' and 'window shopping' are valuable research methodologies in themselves. Always opt to try on garments of interest where possible. This helps to build your knowledge and understanding of technical issues such as fit, contour, fabric, and construction details such as seams and darts, which can all be explored first-hand.

To enhance this experience, always study the garment's fabric label too, so that you can start to appreciate the impact of fabric. Make assessments of what you see and experience, and ideally jot these observations down in a notebook; for example, a garment made from 100 per cent cashmere should feel light, incredibly soft and warm, but you should also note down your own particular thoughts.

Vintage Fairs

Museums can provide a historical overview of fashion through the centuries. While their displays are great for learning about fabric selection and for sketching silhouettes and details, it is very rare that you will ever be given the opportunity to try these garments on. Vintage fairs, on the other hand, provide you with the opportunity to try on 'antique' garments (and sometimes purchase them).

Clothes found at flea markets, garage sales and in second-hand stores can range in age; generally, clothes that are more than 25 years old are classed as 'vintage'. There are also several vintage fairs in the fashion capitals that are frequented by international fashion design teams looking for inspiration, the Clerkenwell Vintage Fashion Fair, the Hammersmith Vintage Fair and the Frock Me Chelsea vintage fair in London, and the Vintage Fashion Fair in Madrid being just a few. Renowned markets such as Kempton, Sandown Park and Portobello Road in Surrey and London, Hell's Kitchen Flea Market and the Brooklyn Flea Market in New York, and the *marchés aux puces* (flea markets) at Porte de Vanves and Saint-Ouen in Paris also continually attract fashionistas, fashion buyers and designers.

Known as a pioneering knitwear designer, Alice Palmer continues to challenge preconceived ideas about what knitwear is. Palmer's ability to push the boundaries of both design and sustainable production methods are notable elements of her label. By integrating both innovative and more traditional methods, Palmer is able to achieve bold garments that are sustainable, sculptural, groundbreaking, ultra-modern and yet completely wearable.

After graduating from the Glasgow School of Art, Palmer studied for a master's degree in textiles, specializing in knit, at the Royal College of Art, London (RCA), exploring and experimenting with unconventional methods for developing constructed knit for fashion. Palmer's focus on sustainability was also nurtured during this time. In a bid to cut down on waste, she explored a method of covering the body by using diagonal shapes, creating V-necks and asymmetric hemlines. Palmer graduated from the RCA in 2007 and set up her own label in 2008.

Inspiration is key to any creative venture, Palmer says. 'For my collections, I am mainly inspired by films, people, art, architecture and nature. I spend a lot of time visiting art galleries in London, including the Schwartz Gallery in Hackney Wick, the Tate Modern and the Whitechapel Gallery ... I have gained inspiration from several different sources and believe that when you combine different inspirations you can create something ultimately more interesting or unique.'

Several collections to date have been inspired by film. The Autumn/Winter 2012 collection 'Vertigo' was inspired by Alfred Hitchcock's classic, in particular the character of femme fatale Judy Barton. Park Chanwook's *Lady Vengeance* inspired Autumn/Winter 2013, a bold, strong collection with references to superheroes and the battle between good and evil. 'I am attracted to superhero movies for the action, humour and narrative progressions,' Palmer says.

Known for her sculptural silhouettes, Palmer comments: 'Normally, I work out the silhouette from the form, or decide upon the form first and then the silhouette naturally follows. However, the silhouette can derive from many aspects of the design process, such as the visual research, the form of the garment or even the negative space of sculpture. ... The sampling and trialling phase is extremely important. You have to be able to visualize the collection as a whole, and the development stage is when you can really experiment and create innovative fabrics and garments.'

Palmer gained international recognition in New York in 2008 when she was awarded Best Womenswear Designer by ASOS. This led to the creation of a diffusion collection, launched by ASOS in the spring of 2009. At the Scottish Style Awards, Palmer was nominated for the Fashion Designer of the Year award in 2009 and 2010, and for the Young Fashion Designer of the Year award in 2011 and 2012. In January 2013, 'Interstellar', Palmer's Spring/Summer 2012 collection, was launched exclusively in Milan at Spiga 2, the Dolce & Gabbana concept store.

*Top left and right
'Interstellar'
collection, Spring/
Summer 2012.*

*Bottom left and centre
'Lady Vengeance'
collection, Autumn/
Winter 2013.*

*Bottom right
'Cirrus' collection,
Spring/Summer
2013.*

5.

Creative Research

Creative research uses primary research techniques. It gives you the opportunity to take out your pencils, paper, pastels, scissors, glue and camera and really explore your theme using drawing, collage and photography. This chapter will also show you how manipulating fabric through deconstruction, customization and draping can help you find new and innovative proportions, shapes and silhouettes.

Art Materials

Whether sticking secondary research resources in a sketchbook, or drawing or painting something that you find interesting, a good selection of art materials is essential throughout the research and design process. There is a broad range of art materials – or 'art media' – available; try to experiment with as many of these as possible as you explore line, form, colour and texture.

For convenience, art materials, excluding your sketchbook, are best kept all together in an art box. Here are a few basic items:

Sketchbook Check the weight of a book's paper by referring to its grams per square metre (gsm), or its basic weight (expressed in pounds). The higher the figure, the heavier the paper. Standard photocopier (text weight) paper is 80 gsm, whereas a postcard (cover weight) is 250 gsm. Sketchbooks are somewhere in between these, ranging between 120 and 160 gsm (around 80–90 lb, or sometimes more). If you intend to use both sides of the pages in your sketchbook, choose a heavier paper to avoid work showing through and interfering with visuals on the other side.

Layout Pad This is generally used during the later stages of the design development process, when trying to maximize the potential of an idea. This item is optional, though; some designers prefer to keep all development in their sketchbook. Layout pads have a gsm of 75 (or a weight of around 16 lb), which means the paper is quite translucent. Similar to tracing paper, this allows copies to be made from an original.

Graphite Pencils These are sold separately or in packs and range from hard to soft, measured on the HB ('hard' and 'black') scale. (The US system rates pencils using a numeric scale – the higher the number, the harder and lighter the mark produced.) The various stages of research and development (R&D) – sketching, design development and technical drawings (or 'flats') – demand a different quality. Sketching often requires softer pencils, whereas designing and technical drawings require harder pencils for clear, defined lines.

Watercolour Pencils These can be used straight from the pack as a dry media, or they can be used as watercolours when blended with a wet paintbrush.

Paints It is advisable to have a tin of watercolours, as well as tubes of gouache or acrylic paints. Both gouache and acrylics can have the consistency of either watercolours or oil paints, depending on how much water is used to dilute them.

Black and Coloured Inks These can be used straight from the jar or mixed with water.

Top
The basic range of media needed for the various stages of research and development. The use of colour in a sketchbook is as important as the use of pencil. The watercolour box set and watercolour pencils are more portable options than the tubes of acrylic and gouache paint when undertaking primary research on field trips. Use a small water bottle for rinses, and tissue to soak up excess water.

Bottom
Graphite pencils are measured on the HB ('hard' and 'black') scale. The mark-making potential of a pencil is dependent on the softness or hardness of the lead.

Paintbrushes Brushes come in a variety of sizes, ranging from the finest detail brush to a large paintbrush. The brush shape can be round, flat, a filbert (oval), a flat blender, long or short, and the bristles can be natural or synthetic; synthetic brushes are cheaper.

Glue You will constantly be sticking primary and secondary imagery in your sketchbook, so finding a good glue for this purpose is important. Glues that are water-based have a tendency to curl and wrinkle sketchbook pages, and the adhesive quality of some is temporary.

Masking Tape This has good adhesive quality, yet it can also be peeled off paper easily. This makes it ideal for securing paper when drawing on an easel. It also provides a non-slippery surface for annotations on sketchbook pages full of imagery. Masking tape is available in a variety of widths.

Eraser Erasers are a useful component in an art box. However, avoid over-reliance on them as a tool; a useful exercise is to practise drawing over mistakes with a stronger, defined line. This helps you see your corrections as your drawing skills improve.

9H 8H 7H 6H 5H 4H 3H 2H H F HB B 2B 3B 4B 5B 6B 7B 8B 9B

Hardest   Medium   Softest

Sharpener or Craft Knife Always have these to hand so that pencil points can be kept sharp.

Technical Drawing Pens These can be used for hand-rendered technical drawings. The tip sizes start from 0.1mm, which achieves a very fine line.

Knowledge of the mark-marking potential of different art materials is essential. You can also experiment with the way you use these materials. For example, a stick of pastel can be used on its side as well as the top edge; gouache paint can be applied with a brush as well as your fingertips. Applied pressure can also be varied. To widen the scope of your work yet further, try experimenting with mixed media.

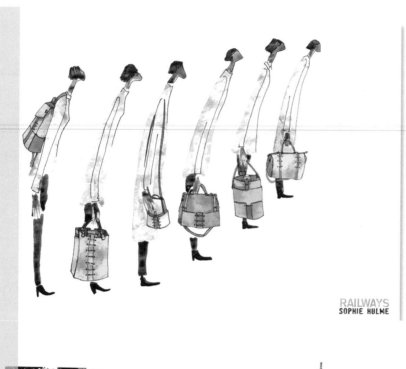

RAILWAYS
SOPHIE HULME

Top
Mixing hand-rendered techniques with computer software such as Photoshop creates images that are polished but not too flat.

Bottom
Knowing your materials will help you get the most out of them. The different applied weights of the pencil marks, as well as perspective and shading, help express the three-dimensional aspects of both the bag and coat.

RAILWAYS
SOPHIE HULME

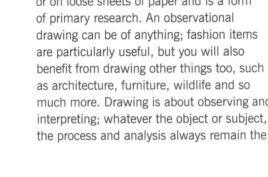

Drawing Effectively

Drawing silhouettes using a continuous line will help you to focus on scale and proportion. Repetition helps too – over time, as you analyse and rework your drawings, your observational skills will improve.

***Observational drawing* is an essential skill.** It is a form of note-taking – it provides a record. It is normally done in a sketchbook or on loose sheets of paper and is a form of primary research. An observational drawing can be of anything; fashion items are particularly useful, but you will also benefit from drawing other things too, such as architecture, furniture, wildlife and so much more. Drawing is about observing and interpreting; whatever the object or subject, the process and analysis always remain the same – interpreting form, line, proportion and balance.

In the research and development process there is an interplay between two-dimensional drawing and three-dimensional realization. The ability to represent an object accurately through drawing requires you to make accurate judgements relating to the fundamentals of design: line, proportion, form and texture.

A useful exercise to try is to draw the outline of an object using one continuous line. Map out the whole object, keeping your chosen media on the paper until the drawing ends where it started. Students often make the mistake of concentrating on one small aspect of a drawing, such as a face, only to find that there is then insuffucient space on the paper for the rest of their subject. By forcing you to concentrate on an object as a whole, this exercise encourages concentration, focus and an understanding of scale and proportion.

Evaluative annotations can also be used to add more depth to your sketchbook. These are explanatory notes, added alongside any drawings, that explore your thought processes and provide explanations and/or assessments of the material. This process is invaluable; it demonstrates an engagement that is deeper than surface level. It shows that thought processes are actively engaged – a skill that is extremely useful for the problem-solving realities of fashion design.

Top
As a representation, there are a few inaccuracies in this sketchbook drawing of a jacket, such as the symmetry of the lower patch pockets. It is essential for effective self-critique that you study your drawings objectively. Making adjustments and corrections is part of the creative process.

Bottom
Drawing garments from life will help improve your three-dimensional understanding of clothing – fit, proportion and silhouette.

At a fashion exhibition, for example, you might draw what you see, exploring drape, textiles, proportion and form, using the contents of your art box to render different fabric types. When adding your evaluative annotations you could ask yourself the following questions: Does the mix of fabrics work – why/why not? Does it remind you of anything else? Does the colour palette work – why/why not? Is the silhouette feminine, masculine – what makes it so? What exactly do you like or dislike about the garment? Recording fabric types, colour palettes and the year and season of any garments will all be useful information for your sketchbook, too.

A/W 1996-97
LONG WHITE DRESS W/ ~~OPEN~~
~~BLACK & BLACK SKIRT~~ HIGH
COLLAR

*Drawing is a form of
note-taking and allows
you to keep a first-hand
record of anything that
catches your eye – like
these drawings, which
were sketched at
the 'Yohji Yamamoto'
exhibition at the Victoria
and Albert Museum
in London. You should
always carry a pocket-
sized sketchbook and,
ideally, use it daily.*

W19
BLACK LONG DRESS
W/ INTEGRATED
SEQUINNED PURSE
ON THE BACK.

S/S '01

CRÊPE DE CHINE,
SEQUINS, METAL &
PLASTIC.

S/S 05

SILK & SATIN.

W7
BLACK HALTER-NECK
LAYERED LONG DRESS
IN HOMAGE TO MADAME
GRÈS W/ PLEAT DETAIL
IN THE FRONT & BLACK
TROUSERS.

Photography

When draping on the stand or on a person, photographs will provide a useful reminder of the individual steps you have gone through while experimenting.

The use of photography as a tool for documentation and communication in the research process is highly recommended. It can not only be used to document a final outcome, but is also an invaluable way of capturing inspiration and generating ideas as you progress through the research and development process.

Photography is very accessible and can involve nothing more than the click of a button; most mobile phones have cameras, and point-and-shoot digital cameras are very easy to use. However, as with anything, experimentation and practice help to build on basic skills.

There are two types of photography – analogue and digital. Analogue photography is the traditional method of capturing an image on light-sensitive film, which is then processed in a dark room to make photographic prints. Digital photography does not use film; it captures and stores images as files for digital processing. When printing off any digital imagery, ensure that the resolution is high – 300 dots per inch (dpi) is the industry standard – to avoid pixelated images. Both analogue and digital imagery can be altered through the use of filters and processing techniques.

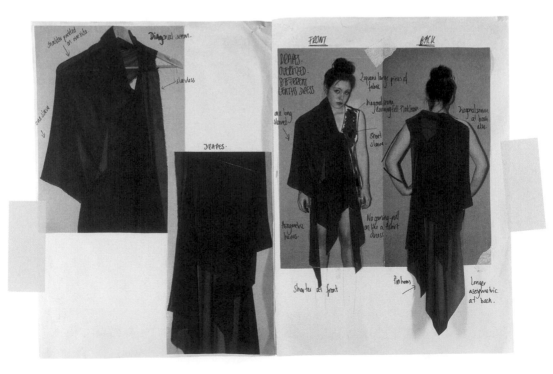

Invest in a small camera that you keep with you at all times so that you are always prepared to capture something inspirational, wherever and whenever you spot it. Anything, from the obvious to the abstract, may prove useful – people, architecture, tree bark, detritus, sunsets, textures, colour compositions are just a few examples. A useful tip for documenting street culture is that most people find smaller cameras less intimidating. And when photographing outside, make sure that the sun is not shining into your lens.

Photography can also be an extremely useful way of recording certain stages of the research and development process, helping to generate ideas that have started to materialize in three-dimensional form. When draping fabric on the stand, for example (see page 114), it is always good practice to photograph each stage of exploration so that you have records to refer back to later.

Photographs provide an invaluable resource when documenting exploration and experimentation. Alongside annotations, they provide a reliable reference source.

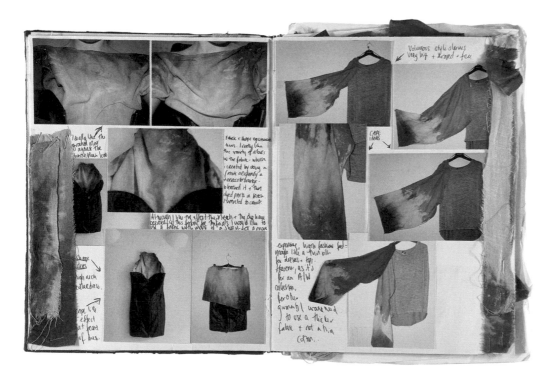

Photocopying

You will often find that photocopies provide an easy way of incorporating secondary research into your sketchbook. However, pages and pages of black-and-white photocopies will make your sketchbook start to look like a scrapbook. Luckily there are several ways to avoid this and to create a sketchbook that is engaging and inspiring, both for you and for any potential viewers.

Experiment with scale by reducing or enlarging any images, and consider using colour printouts as well as black and white. Cutting out any images rather than sticking down whole sheets of paper will also help to break up the effect.

You might also want to explore photocopying on different types of paper. There is a wide variety of paper to choose from, but because it must be fed through the photocopier it cannot be too thick or heavily textured.

- Standard photocopying paper is adequate for photocopying text and black-and-white imagery. There is a tendency for colour photocopies to appear saturated, though, due to the porous quality of the paper.

- Gloss/matt printing paper is the paper used for standard photographs. This quality of paper produces a good representation of colour.

- Brown paper used for wrapping parcels is available both in rolls and in sheet form, and can be cut to any size.

- Sheets of acetate are clear and can be fed through a photocopier. Their transparency helps to create areas of interest in a sketchbook, and can be very useful when overlapping visuals.

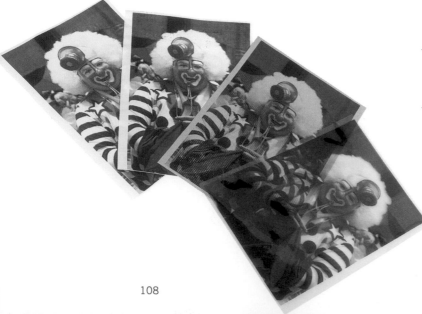

Collage

A *collage* is created by assembling an array of different items or materials, such as newspapers, photographs and fabrics, and then gluing them down together on a piece of paper. Thoughtful consideration of composition, scale and juxtaposition are needed to create a collage that works visually and generates ideas. A sketchbook collage may cover the entire paper surface, or it may consist of isolated elements on a page, with adequate space left for observation drawings, evaluative annotations and initial design ideas.

Collage offers a level of immediacy when exploring the possibilities of scale, silhouette and proportion. Reducing and enlarging the scale of found imagery on the photocopier can often help, too.

ACTIVITY

Create a total of six different fashion-inspired collages using a variety of primary and secondary resources – photographs, drawings, tear sheets and photocopies, for example. Experiment and explore the possibilities of scale, form, texture, details and proportion. Work freely without any preconceived ideas – place no limits on your imagination.

Left
This sketchbook collage has been informed by the silhouette and structure of the toile on the stand.

Right
An outfit has been suggested using collage. This technique will enable you to play with different shapes, exploring proportion, silhouette and balance.

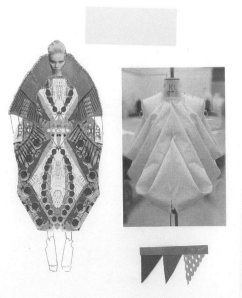

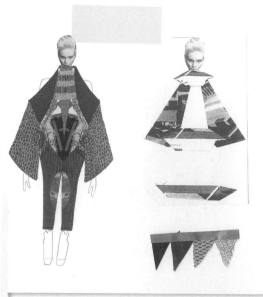

Sampling and Customization

The frill here was originally a cuff detail on a shirt sleeve. It has been used for customization purposes. Three possibilites are explored for the best outcome.

Research is not limited to two-dimensional exploration in a sketchbook. Frequently there is an interplay between two- and three-dimensional practices, and this interplay itself broadens the scope for both research and development possibilities.

With three-dimensional exploration, proportion, form and silhouette become more accessible. Sampling, which involves the three-dimensional interpretation of a specific detail, feature or element of a design idea, is an essential stage. It provides an opportunity for you to realize an idea to see if it actually works, or if you need to go back to the drawing board.

Customization is another example of three-dimensional exploration. It involves changing one or several aspects of an existing garment – the change can be slight or significant. This allows you to challenge the balance of the garment. It can act as a trialling phase in which you consider various permutations that can be used as prototypes – starting points from which other design ideas can flourish.

Deconstruction

***Deconstruction* means taking something apart, whether this is an actual garment or a set of pre-existing ideas.** A garment that has been deconstructed can be reconstructed using a process of experimentation. Prototypes can also be photographed and elaborated upon in a similar way throughout the research and development stages.

As an ideology, deconstruction can provide a methodological starting point. Martin Margiela, a Belgian designer referred to as one of the Antwerp Six – a group of six avant-garde designers who all trained at the Antwerp Royal Academy of Fine Arts in the 1980s – frequently engages in a deconstructive methodology. As a method of research it provides a space to challenge pre-established norms.

A tweed coat has undergone several deconstructive processes. Now the inner workings of the coat have become the exterior.

Deconstruction is used to challenge the purpose and function of a cardigan.

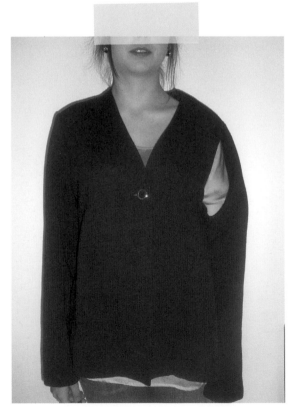

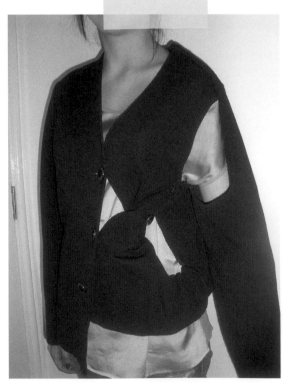

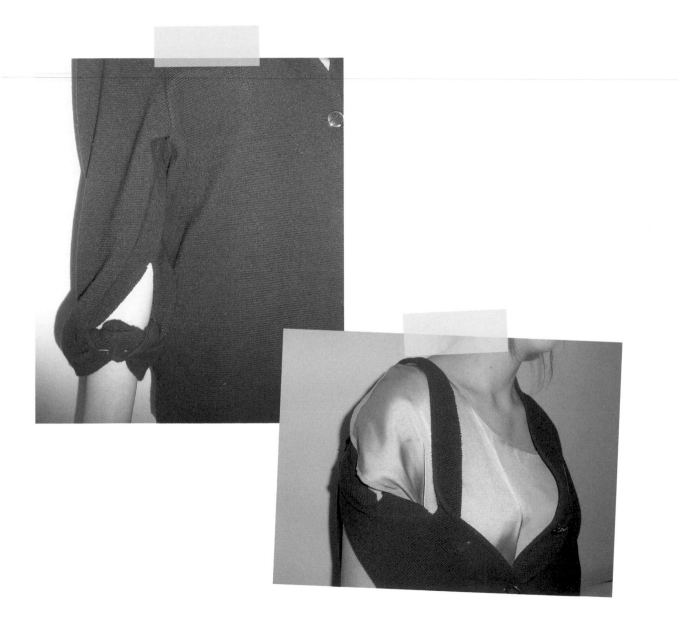

Modelling on the Stand

Left
Modelling on the stand is a very organic process; the chosen fabric often dictates what is achievable – fabric content, weight, grainline and whether it is woven or knitted are all contributing factors. This process can sometimes provide a much quicker solution to a complicated 3D problem than flat pattern cutting.

Right
Working on a mannequin allows you to experiment with scale and the placement of design details, and see how they would work three-dimensionally. Always record your experiments in photos or a sketchbook for later reference.

The three-dimensional exploration of an initial idea, or the qualities of a fabric, can be undertaken very successfully when *modelling on the stand* (tailor's dummy), or draping. In fact, some design ideas cannot be explored fully on paper – this two-dimensional format can be incredibly limiting, leaving lots of unanswered questions. Draping can also be used as a problem-solving tool during development. Patterns can eventually be drafted from prototypes that have been created on a stand.

It is important that you always photograph the various stages of this process, keeping a record that will then inform the research and development process.

Madeleine Vionnet was a renowned draping expert, and is also revered as the creator of the bias cut. Cutting on the bias (on a diagonal as opposed to the straight grain) changes the quality of a piece of fabric, making it more fluid and slightly stretchy. Vionnet was particularly inspired by ancient Greek art, and comfort and ease of movement were fundamental elements of her designs. Her explorations with drape and the bias cut through the use of long lengths of fabric informed her understanding of form, shape and silhouette.

Madame Grès was another designer renowned for draping and modelling fabric to create exquisite garments. Grès had prior training as a sculptor, which greatly influenced her approach to 3D realization.

Top
*Draping has added
fluidity and volume to
this Vionnet creation.*

Bottom
*By modelling on the
stand, Madame Grès
created an intricately
pleated dress.*

CASE STUDY
BLESS

Bless is a conceptual design label, established by Desiree Heiss (based in Paris) and Ines Kaag (based in Berlin). The duo have no fixed rules and their work does not fit into any pre-established category. Instead, they often start by designing for themselves, and have also developed collaborative partnerships with Adidas and Alfa Romeo.

Bless's first collection, 'No. 00 Furwigs', was launched in autumn 1996 with an advertisement in *i-D* magazine. This was spotted by Martin Margiela, who then hired them to make the wigs for his 1997 Autumn/ Winter Paris show. Despite this, the designers remain relatively unknown. 'We are only interested in the work we do and making our child, Bless, known and our values visible so they can be shared by our clients and those around us. We are not interested in gaining notoriety.'

Heiss and Kaag met as fashion students and their early work together revolved around fashion. But by 1999 they were 'slightly bored with fashion and happy to dress things other than the human body', which led to their 'No. 07 Living-room Conquerors' collection, which included three different 'chairwears', a 'tablecare' and a 'doorflair'. Since then they have continued to design multifunctional unisex garments and functional objects. In fact they say that from the beginning they 'questioned the whole fashion industry ... the pace of developing, producing, selling and wearing out did not really match with the expectations we had written down in our manifesto when we imagined our future.'

In line with their rejection of the traditional development methods of fashion design, Heiss and Kaag avoid sketching. Their design process has no general rule: 'Sometimes we start from a conversation, sometimes it follows an email, sometimes a found piece of clothing or object, sometimes a wish from a friend or sometimes we try to solve a problem.'

'We feel most active when we think about how to simply enlighten daily life, ours in the first place, which sometimes brings about products that question old habits, open up routines, break the behaviour of consumption.'

Heiss and Kaag do not see their separate locations as a bar to the development of ideas, either. 'Our partnership is driven by a deep mutual admiration, based on both personal and professional aspects, and sharing both the good and the bad days. Our south German backgrounds mean we share similar values, guaranteeing fast and unambiguous communication, which mainly happens through electronic communication. But we do also teach product design together in Karlsruhe, Germany, so we see each other quite regularly, and we meet in Paris or Berlin during the season and work together when we hold exhibitions. We don't care so much about the geographic circumstances, but try to profit from the very different advantages of our locations.'

6

Fabric Research

For some designers, it is fabrics that provide the starting point for a collection; others source fabrics at a later point, based on what will work with their design ideas. Whichever way you work, an understanding of how fabrics drape and the properties of the individual fibres that they are made from is essential. This chapter looks at natural, synthetic and mixed fabrics, and explains how to choose and source them.

The Importance of Fabrics

Fabrics underpin fashion design – without them, clothes and fashion as we understand them would not exist. A fashion designer with a thorough working knowledge of fabrics is like a sculptor who knows how to mould clay to achieve the best results. Being able to make design decisions based on the handling of a piece of fabric – its weight, lustre, texture and durability – forms an invaluable and essential part of the design process. However, knowledge of fabric suitability is not automatic; it is gradually built up as you gain more experience in pattern cutting and sewing.

Fabrics have a huge influence on how a garment is perceived. Take, as an example, the classic mackintosh and a Levi's jacket. The former is traditionally made from a rubberized cloth and the latter is made from denim, yet both are hardwearing, functional and fit for purpose. If these garments were fashioned out of silk organza your perception of them would be significantly altered. Fabrics can also dramatically change the outline of a silhouette. If both of these garments were made out of silk chiffon, they might prove difficult to construct or recognize in their traditional form.

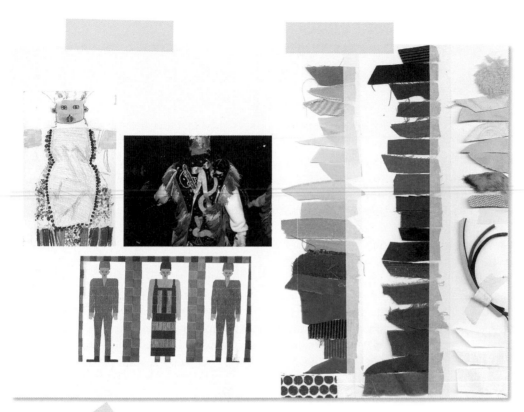

Top
The central image
here has not
only inspired a
technicolour array
of fabrics – it has
also influenced the
choice of fabrics.
The fabric swatches
on the right range
from shiny to fuzzy.

Bottom
Fabric swatches
are displayed on a
page showing design
development. At this
point, the placement
of fabrics is being
considered in terms
of the outfits. Having
fabrics close by in
order to handle them
greatly informs
this process.

Fibres and Fabrics

Fabric retailers stock many rolls of fabric – always ask for assistance if you cannot find what you are looking for. If you describe the sort of fabric you want, sales assistants can often make helpful suggestions.

Opposite page:
Different fabrics have different properties, which will affect the look and feel of a garment. Felted wool (top) cuts with a clean edge, does not unravel or fray and is rigid yet pliable. Cotton (centre) has good durability and utility, is easy to dye and is washable. Acetate (bottom) has a luxurious appearance, a crisp handle, a good drape and dyes and prints well.

Fabric consists of many individual *fibres*. These are spun together so that they form a continuous strand, which is subsequently woven or knitted together with other strands to create fabric. Fibre sources vary, but fibres fall into two distinct categories: natural fibres – which come from animal or plant sources – and synthetic (man-made) fibres. Fabrics in turn can then be made from natural, synthetic or mixed fibres (a blend of two or more different fibres). Time spent familiarizing yourself with different fibres will greatly increase your understanding of their different characteristics.

The use of three different fabrics – wool, cotton and acetate – for three identical skirts highlights the importance of choosing the right fabric for your designs. Each skirt looks completely different, with the lustre, drape and density of the fabric having an impact on the silhouette and aesthetic of each.

The flounces on the wool skirt are much stiffer and, although they hold their shape, they will not flow well in movement. Those of the cotton skirt hang well, but the whole skirt is quite flat in texture. The flounces in the acetate fabric will hold their shape, and are not too bulky. They will rustle in movement and the fabric's sheen will create shade and tone as the light catches the folds.

Your decision on which fabric to choose will depend on your concept/theme/narrative, and the fabric juxtaposition of the final outfit.

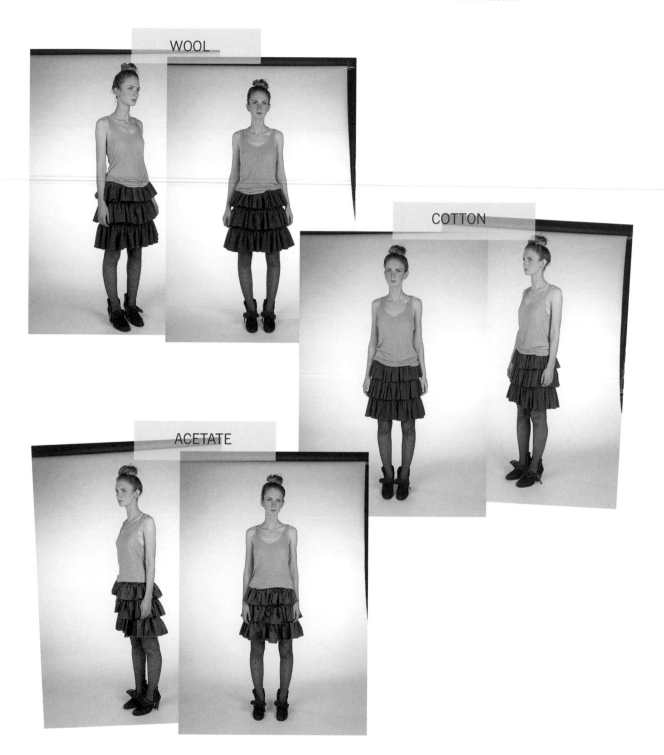

WOOL

COTTON

ACETATE

Fabric Facts –
Natural Fabrics

A *natural fabric* is one derived solely from naturally occurring fibres – for example, animal hair, animal hide, plants, seeds or silkworm cocoons. With all of these apart from the animal hide, the natural fibres are elongated and then spun together to create filaments, thread, yarn or rope, depending on the fibre. These then go through one or a combination of processes – for example, weaving, knitting, bonding or matting – to create fabric.

Natural fabrics are rooted in antiquity. The flax plant, which provides the fibre used to make linen, has been used for cloth for more than 3,000 years. The mummies left in tombs by the ancient Egyptians were wrapped in burial shrouds made of linen, to preserve them after embalming.

Cotton, silk, linen and leather are some of the most widely used natural fabrics today. They vary in their individual properties, but they all allow the skin to breathe, are good absorbers of perspiration, which helps to reduce body odour, and cause fewer allergenic reactions. They are also 100 per cent biodegradable and so are better for the environment, particularly when they are also farmed organically (see Chapter 3).

100% COTTON

100% PURE NEW WOOL

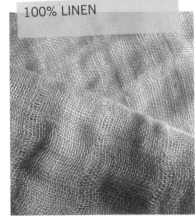

100% LINEN

Top
Yohji Yamamoto
pleated creation
from Autumn/
Winter 2013. Wool
gabardine appears
regularly in his
collections.

Bottom
The Duchess
of Cambridge's
wedding dress, in
ivory satin gazar
with lace appliqué,
designed by Sarah
Burton for Alexander
McQueen.

Fabric Facts –
Man-made Fabrics

A woman hunts for flaws in nylon hosiery laid on a white inspection table, 1948.

The first person to produce a *man-made fabric* was Georges Audemars, a Swiss chemist. In 1855 he patented a fabric called 'artificial silk'. However, the first commercial production of this did not occur until almost 40 years later, using a process invented by the Frenchman Hilaire de Chardonnet, while in England at the same time scientists were developing the 'viscose' method of production. The American Viscose Company began producing viscose in the United States in 1910, and the fabric was renamed 'rayon' in 1924.

The use of acetate for producing cloth – first explored by the American Arthur D. Little – began commercially in 1924 with the Celanese Corporation. Nylon (called the 'miracle' fibre at the time) was developed in the 1930s in the DuPont laboratories by an American chemist, Wallace Carothers.

By 1938 it was being used commercially. The development of nylon was a direct result of World War II, when the importation of silk and cotton from Asia into the US was made virtually impossible and alternatives needed to be found.

Innovation in man-made fibres still continues to offer a level of diversity that is greater than could ever be found in nature, and garments made from silk-like polyester or elastane (spandex), for example, account for a sizeable percentage of the market. Such are the benefits of synthetic materials that they are now used to make high-performance items ranging from super-absorbent nappies (diapers) and surgical gowns, to artificial organs and even building materials for space stations.

Smart fabrics (textiles that incorporate digital components and electronics) also demonstrate the level of innovation in textile technological advances. Shirts that charge phones, clothes that keep the body warm, solar bikinis and much more could become familiar everyday items. An 'invisible cloak', inspired by the Harry Potter books, is being developed and realized by a variety of scientists from countries as far-ranging as Singapore and the USA.

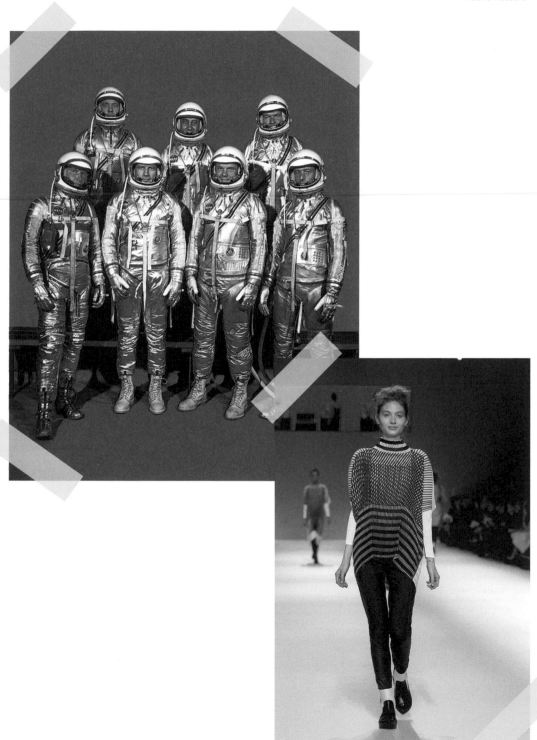

Top
The original seven
Mercury astronauts
in spacesuits made
from a neoprene-
coated nylon fabric
and aluminized
nylon.

Bottom
Issey Miyake is
renowned for using
fabrics that have
undergone some
process that alters
their form. Heat
has been used in a
pleating machine to
create this pleated
polyester fabric.

Fabric Facts –
Mixed Fabrics

***Mixed fabrics* are created when two or more distinct yarns are spun, woven, knitted together or combined in numerous other ways.** Many possibilities exist within this category, with ever more sophisticated blends of fibres appearing on the market. Blends combine the benefits of the individual component fibres. Elastane, for example, is increasingly blended with a variety of fibres to enhance ease and comfort, while the absorbency levels of polyester are increased when it is blended with cotton. When viscose is blended with cotton, the result is a fibre that has much improved softness and appearance.

There are many more examples of property-enhanced blends. By referencing your garment labels you will start to appreciate the full extent of this field.

Textile Terminology

The following glossary covers many of the terms that you will encounter frequently when dealing with fibres and fabrics. Try building upon this list yourself. Form the habit of always looking at garment labels, jotting down any information relating to fabric content as well as your own descriptions of the handle and other general properties in a notebook. In this way you will gradually compile your own comprehensive glossary.

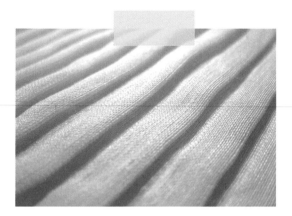

This pleated fabric is a blend of linen and silk. Combining silk with linen reduces the tendency of linen to wrinkle.

Acetate A man-made fibre made from cellulose (derived from wood pulp), mixed with acetic acid. It produces a crisp fabric with a fair amount of lustre.

Acrylic A durable wool-like fabric developed by DuPont in the 1940s. It is soft, inexpensive and does not shrink.

Alpaca A natural animal fibre sourced from the alpaca goat, a member of the llama family. It is a luxuriously soft and warm fibre, with a lustre bearing close resemblance to that of cashmere or mohair.

Angora A natural fibre from the Angora rabbit. It is extremely fine, light and fluffy.

Bamboo A durable natural fibre that has good levels of absorbency and breathability.

Blend A composite of two or more fibres, the combination often offering enhanced characteristics, such as durability, comfort and stain resistance; blends can also be more economically viable to produce.

Botany High-grade wool from the Australian merino sheep.

Camel Hair An extremely luxurious fibre resembling cashmere. It comes from the undercoat of fur that is periodically shed by a camel. It is soft, heavy and durable, and is typically used in smart jackets and coats.

Cashmere Fibres from the undercoat of the Cashmere goat. These produce a lightweight, luxurious fibre.

Cotton A natural fibre sourced from the seeds of the cotton plant. Properties include breathability, comfort and ease of cleaning.

Crêpe Twisted fibres create the crinkled handle of crêpe. Constructed from either natural or man-made fibres, crêpe is lacklustre, with a dryness to the touch. It comes in a variety of weights and transparency levels.

Crimp The natural or artificial waviness of a fibre.

Double Knit A fabric consisting of two layers of looped fabric knitted together to form one heavy fabric.

Elastane (Spandex) A fabric made from elastic fibres that are able to return to their original shape after being pulled up to five times longer. Adds flexibility when blended with natural fibres.

Elastic Yarn or fabric with the ability to stretch.

Embossing A process that involves transferring a design on to a piece of fabric through pressure applied by engraved rollers. The design appears in relief.

Felt The result of layers of fibres compressed to create a compact, non-woven material. Due to the lack of a grain, felt can be cut in any direction without fraying.

Flax A plant fibre principally used in the production of linen.

Foil A pliable metallic layer frequently used in elastane (spandex) and other stretch fabrics.

Geelong The ultrafine hair cuttings from a young merino lamb.

Gin A device that mechanically extracts cotton fibre from the seed.

Hemp Hemp fibres come from the hemp plant, which can grow to up to 6 metres (20 feet) tall. These long and strong fibres are ideal for creating woven fabric.

Interfacing and Interlining These provide an additional layer of material to certain parts of a garment. They are used predominantly for reinforcement, as well as added warmth, durability and shape.

Jersey The generic name given to a knitted garment or fabric. Jersey comes in a variety of natural and man-made fibres, and properties include stretch, robustness and crease resistance.

Jute Jute is a fibrous plant. Its fibres are used to make a plain-weave fabric (also called jute) with a rough surface texture. The fabric is also known as burlap.

Kapok A vegetable fibre derived from the seed pods of the kapok tree indigenous to Central and South America. It is buoyant and water-resistant, and used as a filler in mattresses, upholstery, pillows and life jackets.

Knitting This technique interlocks warp and weft loops to construct a piece of fabric. The warp loops are positioned horizontally and the weft vertically.

Lace An open decorative fabric made by knitting or looping yarns together.

Lambswool The first clippings from unweaned lambs, predominantly used in creating high-grade fabrics. It is a soft, warm, supple and durable wool.

Lamé A fabric made from metallic fibre and traditionally used to make eveningwear.

Leather Tanned animal hide, which dyes easily and comes in a variety of finishes from coarse to smooth.

Linen Fabric made from the fibres of the flax plant. As fabric it is porous, breatheable and cool to wear.

Loom A machine or frame used to produce woven cloth.

Lurex A branded metallic fibre made from polyester and vapourized aluminium.

Lycra DuPont's trademarked elastane (spandex) fibre.

Lyocell A man-made fibre derived from wood pulp cellulose, and belonging to the rayon family. It has good drape, is light, breathable and soft, with a slight sheen.

Mercerization A process first developed by John Mercer in 1844, to give cotton fabric a smooth, shiny surface.

Merino Wool Said to be the best wool fibre in the world. Derived from the Australian merino sheep.

Mesh A very porous and net-like fabric.

Microfibre A man-made blended fibre, the result of weaving very fine polyester and nylon fibre together.

Modal A fabric created from spun beechwood cellulose. It is resistant to shrinking, fading and pilling.

Mohair Fibres from the long hair of the Angora goat. They are strong and durable.

Nylon An abrasion-resistant thermoplastic fibre developed by DuPont since its discovery in the 1930s. It has stretch, is durable, strong and dries with ease.

Pashmina The fibres taken from the soft undercoat of the Changthangi or Pashmina goat of Central Asia.

Pile The yarn that stands higher than the woven base cloth. To achieve velvet or corduroy, the pile is trimmed, shaved and shaped.

Ply To increase the density and weight of a fibre, more than one filament can be twisted prior to being woven. Two-ply indicates that two filaments are twisted; three-ply indicates three filaments.

Polyester A synthetic fibre created from combined polymers. It retains shape well, is strong and wrinkle-free.

Polyvinyl Chloride (PVC) A man-made waterproof fabric.

Ramie A fabric made from the fibres of the ramie plant. It bears a resemblance to linen.

Rayon Refers to a range of man-made fabrics, all made from regenerated cellulose. Rayon drapes well and is soft to handle. See also 'viscose'.

Silk The filament fibre a silkworm produces when creating a cocoon. It is a strong and lustrous fibre that is predominantly used for high-quality garments.

Suede A leather with a velvet-like surface.

Synthetic Man-made and, strictly, not from an animal or plant source.

Tencel A fabric made of cellulose derived from wood pulp. It has silk-like qualities, is soft and drapes well.

Vinyl A fabric resembling leather but made from PVC.

Viscose A regenerated fibre. Although man-made, it is not strictly synthetic, since it is derived from a plant source (cellulose derived from wood pulp). It has great drape and softness and is smooth to the touch. Also known as rayon, or viscose rayon.

Weaving A technique for creating fabric by passing the warp (vertical) and weft (horizontal) threads over and under each other on a loom. How a fabric is woven influences its strength, elasticity, lustre and weight.

Wool Wool yarn is made from hair fibres from a variety of animals, such as sheep, goats, camels and llamas. The nature of woollen fabrics is weave-dependent and can vary greatly, from wool gabardine to wool crêpe and beyond.

Yarn A term that is often interchangeable with 'fibre'. It can be one long natural or synthetic fibre, or the result of twisting several fibres together.

Sourcing Fabrics

Market stall selling a variety of fabrics.

Opposite page: *Students discussing fabric at a wholesaler.*

Fabrics can be obtained from a variety of sources. These include trade fairs, textile mills, converters, agents, importers, stock houses, jobbers and retailers. As a student the majority of fabrics used in your project work will probably be sourced from a retailer. It is, however, possible to build relations with textile mills and other sources too if you approach them. You may also be able to secure fabric sponsorship for your final collection, if not other projects as well. This may be supplied entirely free, or you may be offered heavily discounted fabric from previous season's stock – and occasionally from current stock.

As a designer, developing good relations with fabric suppliers is essential. There are numerous suppliers all competing for business, so choose those that are reliable, competitive, provide consistent quality and meet delivery deadlines.

Textile Mills

Textile mills manufacture woven or knitted fabric. Mills are often associated with a particular specialism, whether this is a specific fabric or process. They offer the most competitively priced fabrics since there is no need for a middleman, although they will require minimum orders. Production minimums, however, are not a static figure and will vary from mill to mill and from country to country, so it is always worth investigating.

Textile mills are keen to show innovation in their fabric lines, so designers past and present have collaborated with fabric designers and mills to achieve exclusive fabrics for their collections.

Agents

Agents, or middlemen, have a very important intermediary role to play in the seasonal cycle. They represent the textile mills on a national and international level by showcasing their fabric collections to both designers and buyers. They also oversee the local and international ordering and delivery of stock. They do not hold stock themselves but are able to showcase fabric collections through the use of large fabric swatches and feelers on **header cards**. Header cards also provide a comprehensive overview of all the different colour options that are available for each fabric.

Importers

Importers buy in fabric from overseas mills in wholesale quantities, which they then sell off in varying quantities. Importers provide a useful service by smoothing out cross-cultural differences (such as language barriers), and they have a good grasp of currency fluctuations. They also assist in all relevant shipping and import-duty documentation.

Wholesalers

Wholesalers sell stock acquired from textile mills and converters (see below). It is important to bear in mind that they do not provide an endless supply of any one fabric, and operate more on a first-come-first-served basis. They often provide a student-friendly environment where fabrics can be bought without minimum requirements.

Converters

Converters buy in large quantities of unbleached and undyed fabrics (**greige goods**) from textile mills, and then have these finished (dyed or printed, for example) by another company before selling them on. Unlike textile mills, converters work on a basis of much smaller minimums, making them more accessible. Collaborations with both textile designers and manufacturers often allow for 'converted' fabrics that are very on-trend.

Jobbers

Jobbers deal in excess stock – they offload mills and manufacturers of unwanted stock. The fabric is then sold off competitively to a wide variety of recipients, from stallholders to retail outlets.

Retailers

The stock provided by retailers can be purchased in any quantity, making this a student-friendly option. This is at a cost though – often up to three times the wholesale price, if not more. Different retailers have different mark-ups, which are reflected in their respective price points.

Choosing Fabrics

Starting fabric research for a project can be quite overwhelming; this can then be exacerbated when in a fabric store surrounded by endless rolls of fabric. Where do you start? How do you know you are choosing the right fabric? Do you ask for cuttings of all the fabrics that interest you, or do you make a definitive selection there and then? How much fabric will you need?

Choosing fabric is a subjective and organic process; designers can have a visceral reaction to a length of fabric. However, this gut reaction is generally based on experience – where learning from prior successes and failures has led to an intuitive feel for fabric selection. In the meantime, applying a methodology to fabric research will guide you through the process.

While in the shop, there are two main areas that you should focus on – concept and colour palette. Always take your sketchbook with you so that you have some initial research to hand, or some visuals that sum up the intended spirit of your collection. Refer constantly to your imagery and ask yourself the following questions to bring focus to your research:

- What season am I designing for?

- Is this a menswear or womenswear collection?

- What types of fabric would work well with my concept/theme/narrative?

- What types of fabric would work well with my silhouette?

- How many fabrics will I need to add interest and bring cohesion to my collection?

- What colours am I thinking of using to create a colour palette?

- What would this textured fabric look like with this shiny fabric? (A question you can apply to any selections of fabric.)

ACTIVITY

Exploring touch and feel is essential for gaining an understanding of fabric types. This activity involves embracing your wardrobe. Set aside an hour a week to go through the various items that you own. Look, touch and try them on. Describe how each fabric feels and drapes in a notebook dedicated to fabric research. Study the fabric content label for any relevant information and jot down your findings alongside your descriptive notes. Repeat this until you have gone through all the contents of your wardrobe.

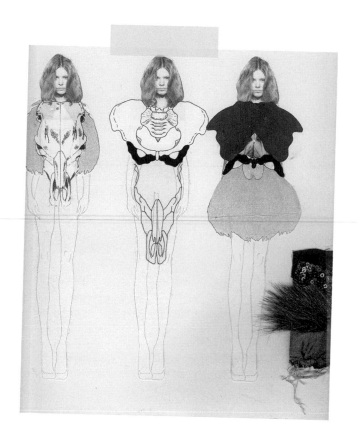

Collecting and Storing
Fabric Samples

Have some fun when combining fabrics to make your selection. There are no rules and, even if there were, rules are meant to be broken. It is best not to have too many preconceived ideas. By making the space to explore and experiment you will have a better chance of creating something fresh and new.

Most fabric stores will provide you with about three fabric swatches on a given day. So, several visits to several stores will probably be needed. Collect as many swatches as possible – fabrics you think might work, as well as those you are sure of. Some shops will sell a length of 20 cm (8 in) as a minimum. This length will give you a better idea of drape, weight and so on than a swatch, but you will need to multiply the cost by the number of samples you need to figure out if your budget will allow for this.

Swatches and purchased lengths of fabric bought from shops and markets can also be used to start your own fabric library. The fabrics should be separated into fibre types for the purpose of easy navigation. Always note down the fabric content of your swatches; with advances in technology it can sometimes be difficult to depend on touch alone when identifying fibres.

Fabric Fairs

Fabric fairs provide a central place where a wide range of fabrics can be bought and sold for forthcoming seasons. They are a notable part of the fashion calendar and the well-known ones always attract international designers and buyers.

Interstoff Asia Essential, IdeaComo and Première Vision (PV) are amongst the most prestigious fairs. Interstoff Asia Essential showcases in Hong Kong in March and October. IdeaComo is held in Milan in February and September. PV takes place biannually in February and September. It follows directly after (though sometimes overlaps the end of) the prêt-à-porter (ready-to-wear) catwalk collections in London, and is probably the most important fair of all.

At a fabric fair professional designers and buyers are typically shown headers by a sales representative of a mill, with the hope that initial sample lengths will be ordered, followed by production lengths. PV opens up to undergraduate and postgraduate students on the last two days of the fair, when complimentary tickets are issued to student groups accompanied by a tutor. Some mills might be willing to part with fabric swatches and catalogues at this stage – it is always worth asking.

Lately there has been a bit of a sea change, and the flexibility inherent in smaller fairs is proving to be a more viable proposition for manufacturers. Whether it is by allowing manufacturers to show off-schedule or providing a more exclusive setting, such as a hotel suite, these smaller fairs are gaining in popularity and attracting more and more international interest.

137

CASE STUDY

ANNE VALÉRIE HASH

Graduating from the Chambre Syndicale de la Couture Parisienne in 1995, Anne Valérie Hash began her career by interning at a number of prestigious design houses – Nina Ricci, Chloe, Christian Lacroix and Chanel. These experiences gave her valuable exposure to the realities of the high-fashion world, from the fitting of garments for couture clients to assisting at catwalk shows. 'I learnt a huge amount, and really came to understand how clothes are made, and unmade.'

Hash's eponymous debut ready-to-wear collection was in Spring/Summer 2001. Her signature style offered a new take on haute couture – infused with a contemporary feel, and in touch with the times. Interestingly, despite the media buzz at the time, not one piece of her collection was sold. Today, the label is stocked in over 120 exclusive outlets worldwide, and is worn by such A-listers as Cate Blanchett, Gwyneth Paltrow, Uma Thurman, Nicole Ritchie and Naomi Watts.

Hash's approach centres on her explorations into the deconstruction of menswear and the subsequent reconstruction process, which results in beautiful, fresh, elegant and feminine womenswear. Fabrics play a role in this: 'I love lace, men's wool suiting, cotton and silk. I love to mix the lace with the masculine fabrics, or to mix the silk with the cotton. I love the association of contrasting fabrics. It is extremely important for me to love and to live the fabric – it is essential. When I touch the fabric I should fall in love. However in my work it's also all about the cut, the cut, the cut.'

Hash cuts, rips and deconstructs garments and fabrics, reconstructing dresses and details such as double collars from a regular pair of men's trousers, for example. 'The feminine/masculine is my first love, with the addition of a level of romanticism in the cut. I love the essence of sensuality over and above the "Sexy Rock Chick" aesthetic.' Her constant play with proportion, and her use of the inside features of a garment – seams, bindings and linings – in some capacity on the exterior are also recognizable elements. Through her unique vision, deconstruction becomes both alluring and practical. Remarking on her methodology, Hash reflects, 'When I started out I often did not know what I was going to find. It was a game and I loved playing with chance. However, today I am more precise, I look for something specific.'

When starting out, Hash's muse was a 13-year-old girl named Lou Liza Lesage, the daughter of friends. Using the tiny frame of an adolescent gave Hash more freedom in her creative exploits: 'When you take adult-sized garments you can reduce them and play with the proportions easily, which you can't on a grown-up.'

In January 2008 Hash became an official member of the Chambre Syndicale de la Haute Couture, which entitles her to call herself a haute couturier. Hash is proud of this accolade and makes a distinction between her house and those such as Chanel and Dior, saying – 'I love the couture mind. I do couture whenever I can, because it takes time to create couture pieces. Couture has evolved and a young generation has emerged.'

Top
Prêt-à-porter
Spring/Summer
2013.

Bottom left and right
Prêt-à-porter
Autumn/Winter
2013 – front and
back views.

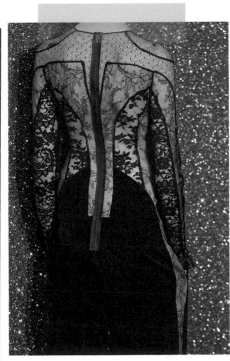

7.

Colour Research

Colour research underpins any fashion collection. This chapter looks at colour theory and colour terminology so that you will be able to apply and discuss colour with confidence. A step-by-step guide to creating a colour palette will also show you how to choose colours that support your concept/theme/narrative in one of the essential developmental stages of realizing your collection.

Colour

We live in an environment saturated by colour – both the natural and the man-made world – and yet the impact that colour has on our lives can often be so subtle that we remain unconscious of it. However, a world devoid of colour would dramatically affect how we make sense of our surroundings.

Numerous studies have confirmed the ability of colour to alter our moods. Certain colours, such as yellow, can improve how we feel, whereas grey can have the opposite effect. Blues and greens, with their association with nature, have been shown to reduce blood pressure, whereas red increases it. Some colours may draw one person in due to their intensity, and yet might repel others for exactly the same reason.

Colour is one of the first things that attracts people to any object. In fact, it takes precedence over shape or detail. Babies and children are more responsive to and stimulated by bright contrasting colours – they help facilitate their learning – and it is from this early stage in our lives that our visual language and an elementary understanding of the world we occupy emerge.

Colour and Fashion

Colour research is pivotal to fashion design. Developing a colour palette for a collection starts at the earliest stages of research and development. During the course of the design process different colours are considered, juxtaposed, mutated, edited and selected through a process of exploration and experimentation.

Fashion is seasonal and so too are the colours used. Designers place a lot of emphasis on creating 'newness', and colour plays a large part in this. All manner of things can inspire a colour palette – for example, photography, travel, found objects, cinema, paintings, nature, vintage textiles, colour forecasting trends; the list is infinite. Climatic changes have a significant influence too. There is a tendency (subject to cultural differences as to how colour is perceived) to favour dark and warm colours during the autumn and winter months because of their ability to retain heat. During the summer months, lighter colours are popular, due to their ability to reflect heat.

An understanding of the basics of colour theory will enable you to make informed choices as a designer. You might want to demonstrate harmony in a collection, and decide that working with muted, nuanced tones will help to achieve this. Alternatively, you may be more interested in conveying an element of tension, and decide to opt for colours that clash with each other. Or, of course, you may be investigating one of a whole range of other possible options in between these two extremes.

Left
Bright, striking colours feature in this Spring/Summer 2003 dress by Alexander McQueen.

Right
Sofia Kokosalaki used gentle pastel tones in her Spring/Summer 2006 collection.

143

Colour Theory

Light is part of an electromagnetic spectrum, which is a broad range of vibrating energies. Only a small percentage of this spectrum is visible to the naked eye – the components of natural white light. In 1666, physicist Sir Isaac Newton (1642–1727) discovered that white light was actually a composite of a range of colours – namely violet, indigo, blue, green, yellow, orange and red. Newton observed that when white light was directed at a solid prism, each of these colours was refracted (bent) differently, resulting in the white light being split into a spectrum, or rainbow.

Colours are detectable by humans when light makes contact with the eye's retina, which is formed of rods and cones. Rods are able to distinguish black from white, and cones are able to detect red, blue-violet and green. The acquired data is subsequently transmitted to the brain and deciphered there, resulting in the colours we see.

A number of colour theorists have explored this subject over the last few hundred years, and all are worth investigating:

- Leonardo da Vinci (1452–1519)
- Moses Harris (1730–ca. 1788)
- Johann Wolfgang von Goethe (1749–1832)
- Philipp Otto Runge (1777–1810)
- James Clark Maxwell (1831–79)
- Michel-Eugène Chevreul (1786–1889)
- Ogden Rood (1831–1902)
- Ewald Hering (1834–1918)
- Albert Munsell (1858–1918)
- Wilhelm Ostwald (1853–1932)
- Johannes Itten (1888–1967)
- Alfred Hickethier (1903–67)
- Josef Albers (1888–1976)
- Faber Birren (1900–1988)
- Frans Gerritsen (1953–2012)

Useful information can also be sourced from the CIE (Commission Internationale de l'Eclairage/International Commission on Illumination), which is the top authority on the subject today.

These theorists' explorations have contributed to the creation of three basic colour systems: subtractive colour, additive colour and partitive colour.

Subtractive colour applies to the mixing of pigments, as undertaken in painting. An object's pigment allows for the absorption of some wavelengths of light, and the reflection of others. The reflected light waves then form the colours we see. When pigments are mixed, the object absorbs more light and so less light is reflected. *Additive colour* applies to the combination of coloured light, and is used in theatrical lighting and television. The *partitive colour* system references a viewer's reaction to colours when they are situated next to each other. The next section will look at colour wheels that represent each of these three basic systems.

Top
Preen, Spring/
Summer 2005.

Bottom
Issey Miyake, Autumn/
Winter 2013

Colour Wheels

A colour wheel offers a way of illustrating colour structures that helps us make sense of how colour reacts and interacts. However, the different practitioners within the creative industries use different colour systems, so their various needs are not met by just one big colour wheel – one size does not fit all.

Painters, for example, use the subtractive colour system to create different colours of paint. They also refer to the partitive colour system for colour placement. Photographers use the additive colour system to explore the colours (hues), lightness and darkness (values) in a photograph, and the partitive system to facilitate reactions and interactions within an image.

The Pigment Wheel

The **pigment wheel** is an application of the subtractive colour system, demonstrating colours produced as the result of mixing. Here, the **primary colours** are red, yellow and blue; these cannot be made by mixing other colours. Primary colours are then mixed to create the other colours of the wheel.

Mixing two primary colours creates a **secondary colour** (green, orange and violet, or purple). Green is the result of combining blue and yellow, orange is created from mixing red and yellow, and violet results from a mix of red and blue. The tertiary colours are the result of mixing a primary colour with an adjacent secondary colour. The tertiary colour achieved is mid-way between the primary and the secondary – for example, when blue and green are mixed, the result is a bluey-green. In the idealized model presented by the pigment wheel, when all the primary colours are mixed together, black is created, although in reality the imperfections of real-life pigments make this impossible.

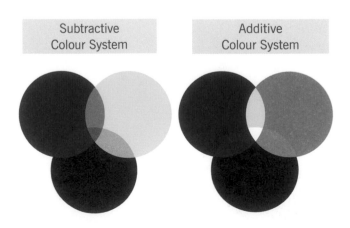

Subtractive Colour System

Additive Colour System

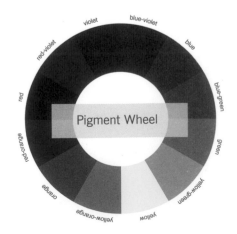

Pigment Wheel

The Light Wheel

The *light wheel* demonstrates the additive colour system. It focuses on how light rays and transparent colour react. The primary colours differ from those on the pigment wheel – here they are red, green and blue. White is created when all the primary colours are mixed together, and black signifies a complete absence of colour. The secondary colours (yellow, cyan and magenta) result from the pairings of red and green, green and blue, and blue and red respectively. This colour system applies to both video and computer graphics.

The Munsell Wheel

The *Munsell wheel* (created by Albert Munsell) follows the partitive colour system. It is used by creatives and businesses working in areas as diverse as interior design, cosmetics and computer hardware. The wheel comprises five primary hues (yellow, red, green, blue and violet). Within the wheel, these primary hues exist in conjunction with after-image perceptions – a process whereby, after your eyes have been fixated on a particular hue derived from nature, your brain reacts by providing the opposite (or *complementary*) hue. The after-image is a second hue resulting from the intense viewing of a primary hue, which is then interrupted by a glance at a white surface.

Blue-green is the after-image when red is viewed intensely. Blue-green also acts as a complementary hue to red, as does the after-image of blue-violet to yellow, red-violet to green, and yellow-green to violet. These are positioned opposite each other on the Munsell wheel.

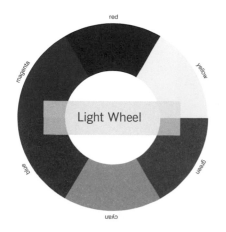

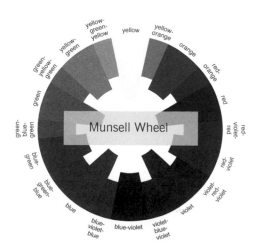

Colour Terminology

Familiarizing yourself with the appropriate colour terminology will further enhance your understanding of colour. As the previous section showed, the definitions of primary, secondary, tertiary and complementary colours will vary depending on the colour system used. The pigment wheel (subtractive colour system) is of most use to fashion designers and is consequently referred to (though not exclusively) in the overview of colour terms below.

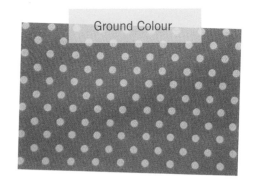
Ground Colour

Primary Colours Red, blue and yellow. These cannot be created by mixing any other colours.

Secondary Colours Green (yellow mixed with blue), orange (red mixed with yellow) and violet (red mixed with blue). These are the result of mixing two primary colours together.

Tertiary Colours Created by mixing a primary colour with an adjacent secondary colour; the tertiary colour takes on an appearance somewhere between the two.

Complementary Colours These colours are positioned opposite one another on the colour wheel. They are very dynamic when placed next to each other – for example, red next to green, orange next to blue, or yellow next to violet.

Harmonious Colours These colours are situated close to each other on the colour wheel; for example, reds and violets, or blues and greens.

Analogous Colours Analogous colours create harmony within a colour palette. They are colours that are adjacent to each other on the colour wheel.

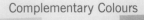
Complementary Colours

Analogous Colours

Cool Colours Shades of blue and whites are good examples of cool colours. Cool colours are often derived from natural phenomena such as the sea, snow, water and sky, and associated with cold conditions.

Warm Colours Nature also provides a good reference point for warm colours; reds and yellows are evocative of fire, sunlight and warm weather.

Neutral Colours Colours such as beige, olive, khaki, grey and brown. They are based on the tertiary colours.

Subdued Colours Colours made less vibrant with the addition of black, grey, white or a complementary colour. The resultant colour is subsequently either shaded up or down, appearing darker or lighter than the original.

Ground Colours This is the hue, shade or tone that represents the majority of the background of an object or image.

Accent Colours A hint of colour that makes an impact.

Pigment Coloured powder used for making paints, inks and dyes.

Hue The name attributed to a colour, for example green, purple and yellow, independent of its brightness or intensity.

Intensity, Saturation or Chroma The level of intensity a hue has due to its purity and saturation of colour. For example: red (high intensity) versus pink (low intensity).

Value Relates to the brightness of a hue – how light or dark it is. For example: orange (light) versus brown (dark).

Gamut A range of a colour that can be accurately reproduced by a particular device or set of pigments – the gamut will vary depending on this. This accounts for the discrepancy between the colour seen on a computer screen and that of a printed-off copy.

Tint Mixing a colour with white creates a tint.

Shade Mixing a colour with black creates a shade.

Tone Mixing a colour with grey creates a tone.

Achromatic Greys The result of mixing black and white together.

Chromatic Greys Greys with low saturation of a hue.

Greyscale Within computer terminology, an image in greyscale is an image composed of tonal variations of achromatic greys.

Monochromatic Featuring a tonal range of just one hue For example: a sepia-effect photograph shaded with brown.

Contrasts Colours that are frequently in opposition on the colour wheel. When paired together the strong difference is evident.

Colour Palette Within fashion, the range of colours used within a collection.

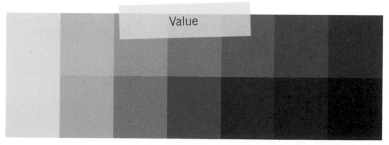

Value

Colour
Perception

Prussian blue, chartreuse, eau de nil, pumpkin, blush, boat green, mushroom, indigo, flamingo pink, sage, taupe, Persian red and fawn are just a few colour names from an infinite list. Colour as an adjective has a powerful impact, whether it is used to differentiate garments or to describe the differences between hues of paint.

The perception of colour is highly subjective. Variables such as the light under which colour is experienced – daylight, fluorescent, electric – have a huge bearing on how it is perceived. Also, the environment that a colour is situated in is important – any colour will be experienced differently, for example, if it is paired with a dark as opposed to a light colour, or placed next to a colour that is opposite rather than adjacent to it on the colour wheel. The surface of a piece of coloured fabric will have a huge bearing on how that colour is experienced too, since different surfaces absorb and reflect light waves differently. Black suede, for example, will appear darker than black patent leather; the first material absorbs more light waves whereas the second reflects more.

Communicating Colour

Clearly the subjective perception of colour is a disadvantage in any type of industry dependent on the accuracy of colour, and the fashion industry is no exception. Different garments within a collection are often manufactured in different factories – and often different countries – and subjected to different conditions. What is there to guarantee that the textile mills, the designer and the retailer are referencing exactly the same colour when referring to 'tobacco' or 'cobalt', for example? The margin for error is huge when such variables as colour perception, subjective interpretation, light and fabric types have such a considerable impact on how a colour is experienced, and colour names alone are not enough.

Very good communication between the different levels of the fashion supply chain is therefore of vital importance. A system of standardized colour referencing is also crucial. There are several colour classification systems used by the fashion and textiles industry, the most popular being the PANTONE® Fashion + Home and the SCOTDIC (Standard Color of Textile Dictionnaire Internationale de la Couleur) systems. Both systems are derived from the emphasis placed on hue, value and chroma by Albert Munsell, as indicated in the Munsell wheel (see page 147), and they catalogue a vast array of individual colours, coded for precise identification and colour matching.

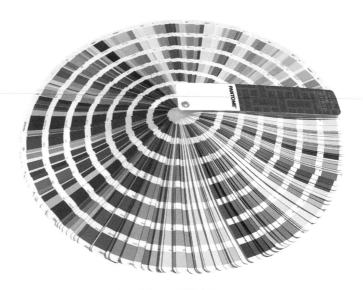

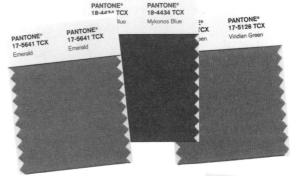

How to Create
a Colour Palette

*The fabric swatches
on this sketchbook
page have replicated
the tonal variations
evident in both
images. At some
point during the
design development,
this current colour
selection will be
edited down.*

A *colour palette* is a range of colours used exclusively within a fashion collection, a painting, an interior or similar. Creating a palette can be a lot of fun; time spent experimenting with colour through random play is extremely good practice, and often results in fresh and exciting combinations. Fashion is about 'the new', so the nuances of a colour – shade, tone or intensity – when combined with those of other colours must be constantly revisited, broken down, assessed and reconfigured to keep everything contemporary.

As mentioned earlier in this book, a good designer needs to remain aware of their environment and constantly be on the lookout for inspiration. Colours are rarely experienced in isolation, though; they are normally seen adjacent to other colours. The colour combinations that surround us everyday are always informative, but they should also be challenged in the search for new perspectives.

Your own colour library can also provide a good jumping-off point when trying to devise a colour palette. This library can consist of disparate objects of colour, as long as they are inspiring. You can continually add to this library, and review its contents with fresh eyes as you compile each new colour palette.

The colour palette of a collection is intrinsically linked to the mood and feel of the collection. A collection inspired by the circus, for example, might require a palette that exudes a sense of fun, energy and excitement. On the other hand, a collection based on purity might be based on the nuances of a single colour. Here, though, you would need to experiment with these nuances to devise a palette that worked effectively.

Start a colour library for future reference, and devise a storage or filing system that will be easy to navigate. Content can be devised to suit your purposes, and may include anything from tear sheets to fabric swatches, yarn, postcards and found objects.

A decaying urban cityscape and interior with graffiti evident have inadvertently inspired a light and breezy colour palette.

Step-by-step Guide to Creating a Colour Palette

There are several different ways of creating a colour palette. The following steps outline just one possible route.

- Can you identify any recurring colours in your gathered primary and secondary research imagery? Make a note of these. Collate them and put them to one side.

- Write down a list of words that best describe the concept, mood, theme, narrative or inspiration for your collection.

- Write down a list of colours that you feel best sum up the concept, mood, theme, narrative or inspiration (do not forget that this is your own personal interpretation of events).

- Go on a hunt for materials such as fabrics, found objects, yarns, scrap paper and paints (with which you can manually create colour) that work as examples for the colours under consideration. Your colour library will be a great place to start. Collate them and put them to one side.

- Colours can also be created through a variety of dyeing techniques.

- Bring together the evident colour/colours from your primary and secondary research investigation with the colours representative of the concept, mood, theme, narrative or inspiration.

- Play.

- Reference the colour wheels for further ideas. Investigate how applying harmonious, analogous or complementary colours (for example) to your pre-existing colours might work.

- Decide on how many colours you want for your collection: too many colours can lead to a disparate-looking collection, and yet too few colours can result in a lacklustre one. A collection needs to be cohesive.

- Continue to play. Photograph or document through hand-rendered techniques the various colour-combination propositions.

- Separate the more successful propositions from the not so successful.

- Sleep on it or review propositions after a coffee break – it is imperative to create some distance so that you can revisit with fresh eyes. Then make your decision.

- A colour palette has a tendency to evolve just as design does in the research and development phase of a project. It is essential to allow this process to happen; design is best when it evolves organically.

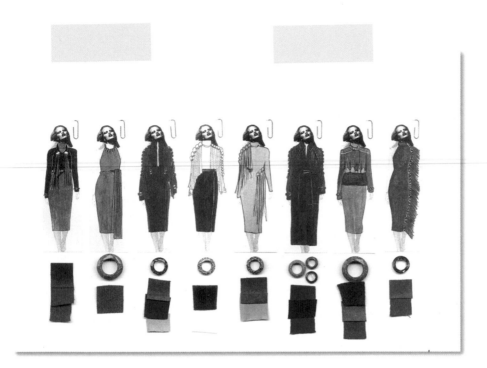

Top
A final line-up showing the use of a colour across a collection. The fabric swatches and the coloured accessory details indicate that this student has really worked at finding the right colours.

Bottom
A colour palette can consist of subtle colours.

155

Colour Distribution

It is essential that you pay particular attention to the balance of colour across a collection. This will provide a sense of cohesion to a group of garments that might otherwise seem disparate. Colour distribution can also help to emphasize a collection's concept, mood, theme or narrative. Take the example of a colour palette that uses black and white. There are an infinite number of possibilities as to how these colours can be distributed and the concept conveyed. The balance of this duo could on one hand evoke Bridget Riley's 1960s Op Art, or it could reference Goth subculture, with white used to accessorize.

This practice should not be left to the end but explored constantly throughout the design process. All the outfits should be complementary, fitting together to form a whole – the collection – that is greater than the sum of its parts.

The creation of a colour palette and how colours are distributed across a collection is affected by personal taste. The rules of yesterday about which colours you cannot mix together – navy with black, or white with cream, for example – are there to be broken in the rule-less world of today. In capable hands any colour combination has the potential to work.

It is important, though, to be mindful of the effect that colour can have on skintone. Some colours can be unflattering, making their wearers look pasty and unwell. This knowledge might influence where you place certain colours within your collection – you may choose to use them away from the face, for example on trousers or skirts, or as an accent colour, whereby use will be minimal.

Top
*Once you have
created a colour
palette, the next
step is to explore
how best to use it
in your collection.
For this collection
of ten outfits, two
different colour
distributions are
proposed.*

Bottom
*A sense of harmony
and cohesion is
achieved through
the balancing of
pastel colours in
this collection of
clean lines.*

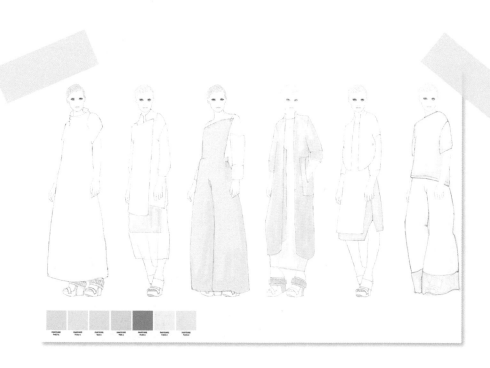

Colour Forecasting

There are many different types of designers and design companies. Some prefer to create their own colour palettes in response to colours that have developed through their own active research, whereas others create palettes by referencing colour trends stipulated by *colour forecasters*.

The role of a colour forecaster involves making predictions about consumer and market-sector 'moods' or palettes of colour preferences up to two years in advance, based on a thorough examination and interpretation of social and cultural events. Colour forecasters do not dictate which colours the fashion industry must use; they simply gather global data on sales figures and changes in attitude to colour in order to predict what customers are likely to buy in two years' time.

A global perspective on trend forecasting is achieved through biannual conferences held in the US and Europe, and attended by an international mix of world-leading colour consultants. These consultants – the Colour Group and the International Colour Authority (ICA) of the UK, and the US-based Color Marketing Group (CMG) and the Color Association of the United States (CAUS) – make their forecasts based on years of experience, strong observational skills, a tacit understanding and sales figures. As an example, colour forecasters understand that colours can frequently be a response to societal economic peaks and troughs. In times of austerity, traditional, sombre colours are popular, whereas bright, energetic and interesting colours sell more in times of greater prosperity.

Première Vision, the biannual Paris fabric fair, displays forecasted trends in both colour and fabrics for upcoming seasons. Forecasted colours are frequently ready for distribution by dye companies up to two years in advance of the retail selling season. As with clothes, there are also fashions in colour – some colours have more staying power, while others are more of a fad. Autumnal colours have a tendency to appear for the Autumn/Winter season, while pastel colours usually appear for Spring/Summer.

CASE STUDY  ERDEM

Erdem Moralioglu was born and raised on the outskirts of Montreal, Canada, by his British mother and Turkish father. Memories of designing and making tiny blue dresses for his twin sister's dolls are vivid recollections of his childhood years, and were the first seeds of what has become a successful career in fashion design.

Moralioglu relocated to Toronto to study fashion design at Ryerson University, then after graduation he decided to move again – to the UK, a place full of history and extended family, and which held a certain romanticism for him. Moralioglu secured an internship at Vivienne Westwood in London, where he gained an insight into the day-to-day realities of an iconic brand, then in 2001 he began studying for a master's degree in womenswear at the Royal College of Art, with a scholarship from the British Council. 'Completing my master's at the RCA was a hugely important experience since it was there that I really figured out who I was as a designer.'

After graduating from the RCA, Moralioglu was snapped up by the Diane von Furstenberg label and subsequently moved to New York. However, after a year in New York, he decided to return to London in a bid to crystallize ideas he had of running his own fashion label. In 2005 the Erdem label was launched at the prestigious Fashion Fringe competition show, where he was awarded first prize, and secured two accounts – at Harrods and Ashley's Boutique.

The Erdem label is now sold worldwide at prestigious outlets, and worn by high-profile customers such as Tilda Swinton, Sienna Miller, Thandie Newton, Michelle Obama, Samantha Cameron, Chloe Sevigny, Keira Knightley, the Duchess of Cambridge and Claudia Schiffer. According to Moralioglu, the Erdem woman 'is someone strong yet still feminine. She's intelligent, independent and follows her own convictions. She marches to the beat of her own drum.'

The use of colour within elaborate prints is an identifiable signature of the label. Colours are juxtaposed with others as if by accident, while still achieving a sense of harmony and balance. Moralioglu comments, 'I believe one of the most important things as a designer is to create your own language, something others recognize as yours. Colour and textiles are part of that for me but so is adding a human hand to my work, whether that means a touch of embroidery or delicate hand-made lace.'

As a child Moralioglu apparently became fixated with the colour blue, and refused to wear any other colour. Although his palette is now more extensive, this passion for colour has not waned: 'I love colour and experimenting with it; it is a very important aspect of what I do as a designer and something I've never been afraid of. I've always found black to be more difficult than colour. There are many factors that lead me to the colours I use. I like the idea of contrast, so each season's colours tend to be a reaction to the previous collection. For example, the Spring/Summer 2012 collection had a soft, pale palette and then Fall was predominantly composed of strong, saturated jewel colours.'

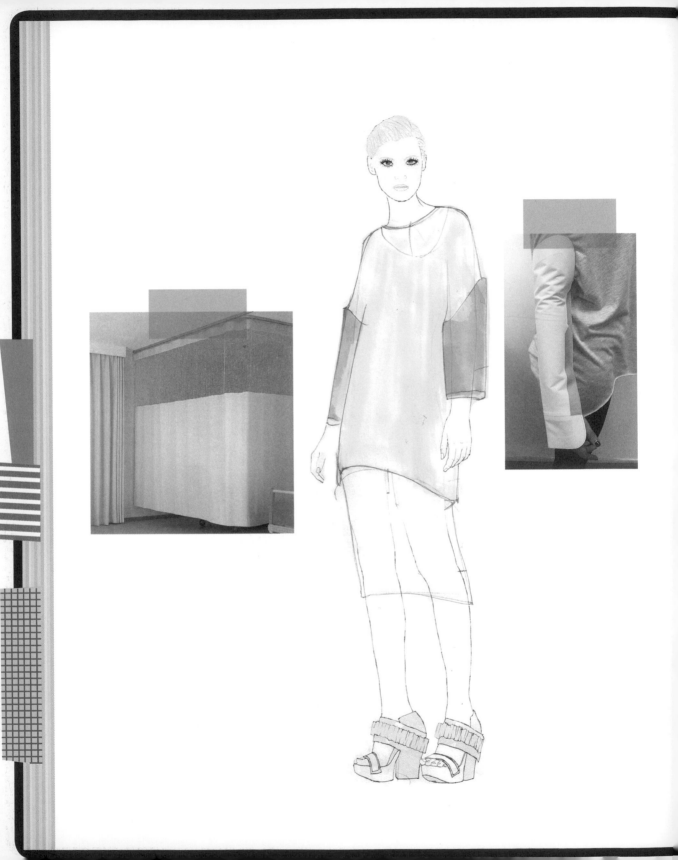

As you gather together all your creative and informational research, you need a strategy to make the most of it all. This chapter explores how to draw out your design ideas using triangulation, how to analyse them and how to edit them down. We will also look at the creation of mood boards, the design development process, and producing finished presentation sheets for your portfolio.

Triangulation

These two dress designs are the product of triangulation between the image of the caravan and the red fabric swatch. The corrugated surface of the exterior of the caravan has inspired the suggestion for a print design on the dress on the left.

Triangulation, as we saw in Chapter 2, refers to utilizing two or more sources to validate a piece of information. Within visual research, triangulation is about collating primary and/or secondary imagery, finding links that will lead to an initial design idea. Good triangulation is evident when the initial design idea brings together several strands, so two or more sources are vital, and your sketchbook should show evidence of your development process. Relying on a single source can create a painting-by-numbers approach, in which all the elements of one research visual are literally copied, transferred and integrated into an initial design idea with little evidence of transformation.

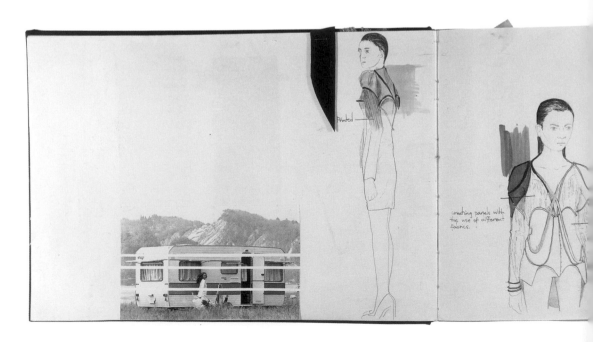

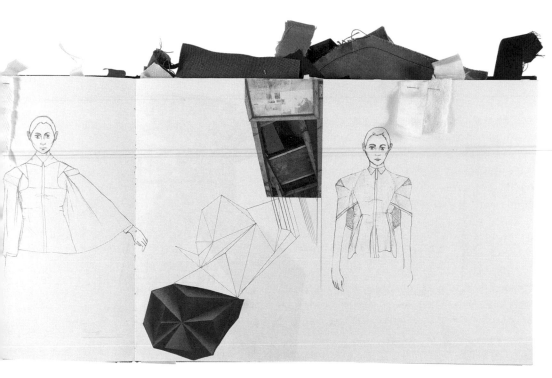

Top
The design ideas here have been heavily influenced by the geometric images, both in the proposed silhouette in the suggested sleeve detail and also in the seams and darts that cleverly create a sense of geometry in the main body of the shirt.

Bottom
Triangulation of elements evident in the statue's attire and the knot diagram are explored in the initial designs on these sketchbook pages.

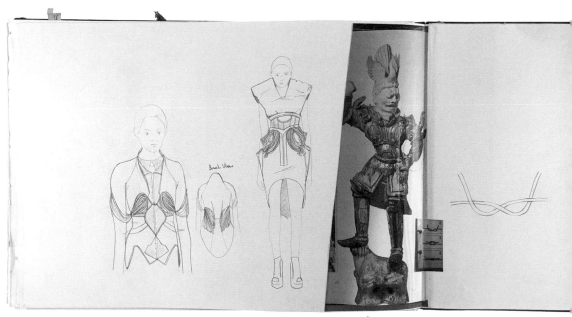

These sketchbook pages show an investigation into the range of procedures used to distress fabric. Fabric plays an important part in design, and investigating the properties and durability of any proposed fabrics will enable you to make more informed choices.

An Investigative Approach

An investigation is a thorough examination; it will reveal information via a process of enquiry. An investigative approach will help you to uncover layers within your research, enabling a deeper level of engagement with your subject matter. Looking for areas of complexity that can at first remain hidden under the surface can greatly benefit the integrity of your final designs.

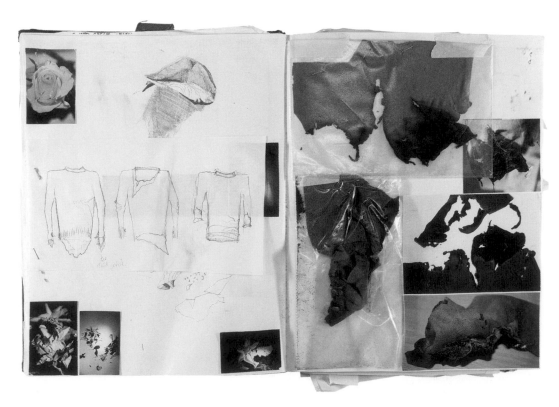

Capsules and Vessels

Chloé

Top
Drawing garments from life is one of the best ways to investigate how a garment fits and how fabric drapes. Drawing from life gives you a good understanding of three dimensions.

Bottom
These sketchbook pages document an investigation into the use of stripes, exploring the changes they can undergo when subjected to folding, tucking and gathering. When considering the use of stripes in a design, width and direction are important factors, so a thorough investigation is key to thoughtful application.

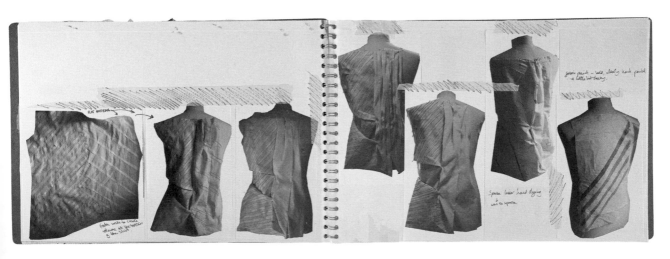

Here, two secondary images show two extremes of necklines. The initial design ideas then explore what is possible by taking various aspects from these images and reconfiguring them.

Interplay Between Images

Looking for links between research visuals is a useful and rewarding activity. Links can be about establishing complementary elements between different images as well as identifying opposing elements (juxtapositioning). In both instances the result will be a widening of design possibilities. During the early stages of collecting research visuals, refrain from sticking them into your sketchbook. Take some time to assess the imagery gathered first; by aligning similar and opposing types of images, new fields of enquiry might unfold. The more disparate your research imagery is, the greater the range of possibilities it will present.

Initial Design Response

There is always a reason behind choosing an image for research purposes; a certain level of interest has drawn you to it. This interest can be either positive or negative. You do not have to like all the images that you choose; the main thing is that you are able to glean something of use from them. This can range from a particular tone of a colour to the intricate design of a brocade detail to a silhouette suggestion. In theory, every chosen image should elicit a design response.

When a selection of images are spread across the sheets of a sketchbook, the links between the imagery create the space for an initial design response. Even if this is just the idea for part of a garment or a detail, make a note of this in the form of a sketch, ideally supported by annotations.

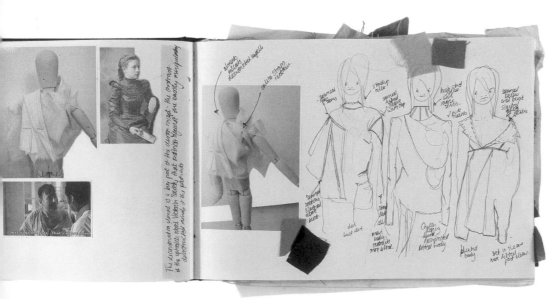

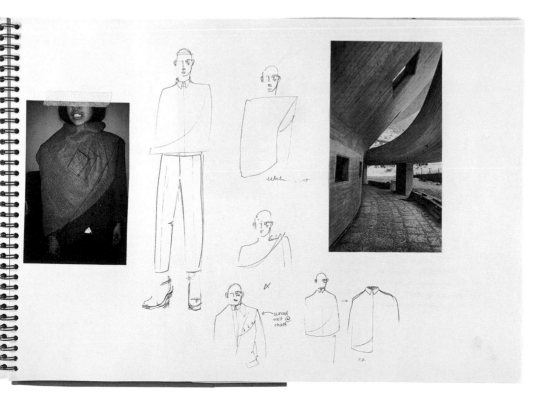

Top
A photo of a man with dreadlocks has influenced the design drawings on these sketchbook pages. The dreadlocks have been reinvented and made relevant as a fringing detail in the designs.

Bottom
An architectural image, with its sweeping curves, has inspired a number of responses: a 3D realization of a garment that, by integrating a sweeping curve, has become an asymmetric garment, and some sketches that suggest the possible use of a curve within the design of a shirt.

Analysis

Below and opposite
An analysis of
volume and fit is
being carried out
on these sketchbook
pages. Working
with an over-sized
garment on a fellow
student, a variety
of propositions are
suggested, analysed
through evaluative
annotations and
then acted upon
in the initial design
drawings.

Analysis involves breaking something down into its constituent parts to make sense of it. To be able to carry out a logical, objective analysis you will need to maintain an element of detachment and objectivity. The process of asking the right questions is important if proper investigation is to take place, and these will not become apparent if you approach the task with an overly subjective viewpoint.

Analytical Skills

Inherent to design is the ability to problem-solve, and this is greatly aided by good analytical skills. To improve your skills you must continually ask questions of yourself and your endeavours, such as:

- Why am I doing this?
- What do I hope to find?
- Are the findings relevant?
- Can I draw any conclusions from the findings?

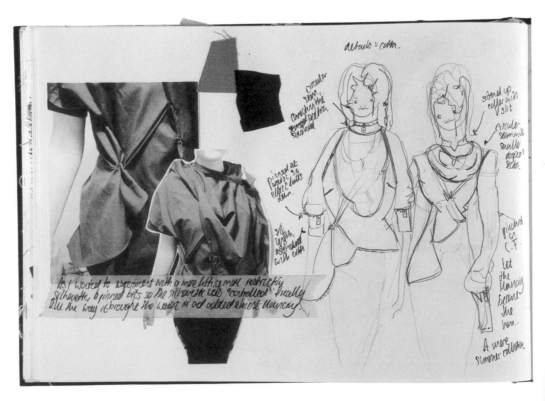

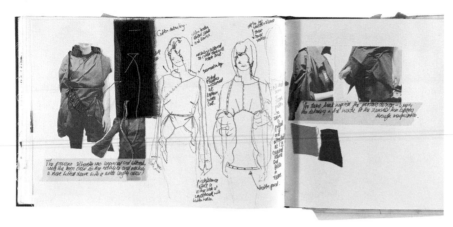

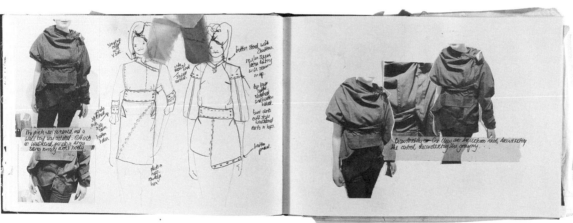

Editing

Mood boards represent a fine edit of all your existing sketchbook research, and an overview of the concept of your project, so that you can refresh your memory at a glance. This mood board has been composed in Photoshop and will form part of a portfolio of work.

As with the notion of a trend (Chapter 3), a 'funnel' metaphor is very useful for visualizing the breadth and depth of research and design occurring at different stages of the design process.

The mouth of this funnel is broad, and represents the scope of all the gathered primary and secondary research materials under investigation during the initial stages. There is no editing at this stage – 'more is more'. It is crucial to maximize all possibilities. Further along the trail, when links between primary and secondary resources start to become apparent, there is a narrowing of the funnel. Connections are now being made, both mentally and visually, resulting in initial design ideas. Finally, we reach the 'less is more' stage, represented by the narrow stem of the funnel. At this point a particular facet of your research has been established as the main focus. The latter stages of the design process are both narrower and deeper.

There is an inherent process of elimination in making decisions while researching, and this is known as editing.

Editing Skills

Not all collected imagery will be relevant to the task at hand. Try to remain objective and ask questions of your work so as to weed out the red herrings. Why do you have this image? Is it relevant? Can it be used as a reference for a colour palette, ambience, silhouette, form or proportion ideas? What links are being made? Are you gathering some momentum? Are you thinking of initial design ideas? Do you simply have a sentimental attachment to a particular image – is that the only reason it has made the edit?

It is important to note that images that are edited out during this process of elimination can often be useful in future projects, so do not discard them completely.

SELECTED
HOMME

Top
The shirts illustrated
here have been edited
in – they have been
deemed successful in
conveying the design
concept.

Bottom
Hussein Chalayan,
Spring/Summer 2003.
An initial design idea
that has made it to
the catwalk.

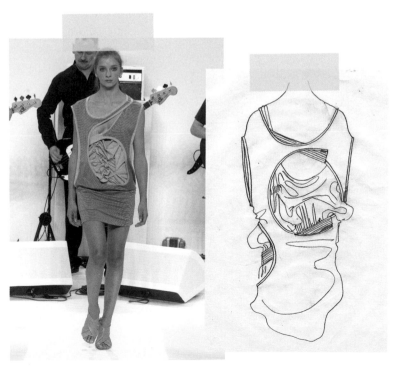

What to Do When You Are Stuck

Top
Repeat visits to the library can kick-start you into action again when you are feeling unmotivated.

Bottom
A student's desk has been personalized with current research imagery.

Encountering a creative block, when the flow of relevant ideas seems to stall abruptly, whether momentarily or for longer periods of time, can be very disconcerting and give rise to self-doubt. However, it is important to remember that blocks can occur at any time, and to any creative. Design is rarely a smooth trajectory to an intended outcome; a rollercoaster ride, full of peaks and troughs, is a better metaphor. In fact, these periods of self-doubt are not even always negative. They can often provide the opportunity to re-evaluate, re-energize, reconnect and re-focus.

However, the following is a list of strategies that you may want to try the next time you are faced with a creative block. Some of them may seem more like methods of procrastination, but it is important at these times to allow yourself to indulge in something that is guilt-free, enjoyable and brings about a relaxed state of mind.

- Persevere. Continue working. It might be preferable to carry on, rather than go through the pain, discomfort or angst that you may experience if you give up. Perseverance might help to unlock the potential in your ideas.
- Utilize your time efficiently by transferring your attention to another aspect of the research and design process
- Sleep on it. You will hopefully view things differently tomorrow.
- Stimulate your mind. Listen to music.
- Get some fresh air. Go for a walk.
- Do some relaxing sketches in the park
- Catch up on some reading
- Go away for a weekend
- Sit outside a café and do some people-watching
- Go back to the library
- Go to the gym
- Take a long shower
- Create some order in your workspace
- Go for a bike ride
- Look through past work
- Talk. Engage in a conversation.
- Practise some yoga
- Go vintage shopping
- Go window shopping
- Go to an exhibition
- Go to the cinema
- Go to the theatre
- Go out dancing.

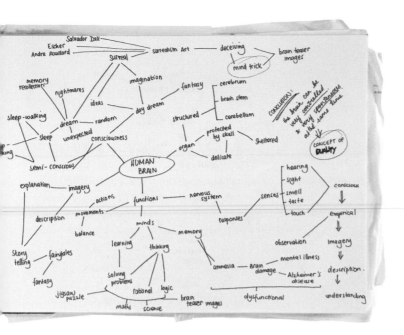

Spider diagrams can be referred to at all the different stages of research and development.

I can have a problem with having too many ideas and not knowing when to stop feeding off my research. When that happens I stop and edit before I get too ahead of myself; I work on the ideas I already have and take them into development.
Tami Soji-Akinyemi

If I'm stuck I'll go and find some fresh imagery, do some detailed observational drawings from the research, and hope a new direction and design ideas come.
Bradley Snowden

I always go back to making samples of fabric techniques or details. The possibilities with materials are endless and this somehow always manages to kick-start something new and open up the process again.
April Schmitz

I get some fabric and work it out on the stand until I get the inspiration to move forward.
Alice Fern

I usually review my ideas (usually by creating a second and/or third mind map) just to emphasize the whole concept to myself again. Because I sometimes lose track of the initial concept during the development process, the review acts as a reminder. From the mind maps, I sometimes find different perspectives on how to view the concept, too. Working on the stand is also very useful, seeing how the fabric could relate to and support the concept.
Danya Sjadzali

I start to collage a few images together, and from there I find interesting ideas.
Tracey Sampson

Mood Boards

Once you have begun to edit down your research you will then be ready to create a mood board. Within fashion design, concept boards, mood boards and storyboards are all essentially the same thing – they provide a summary of a collection, in which the themes, inspirations, concepts, colours and fabrics are communicated to the viewer. Unlike a sketchbook, where a visible development process is an essential element, mood boards work best when careful editing has taken place and artistic expression is displayed in a considered composition.

The gathered images are assembled and then mounted on a board. The size of this may vary – A4 (8½ x 11 in), A3 (11 x 17 in) or sometimes larger, A2 (17 x 22 in) for example. For presentation purposes, however, it works well if all the work done for a particular project is of the same size.

How to Create a Mood Board

To compile a mood board, an assessment of all research materials needs to take place. From the array of imagery, fabrics and other materials collected, select the most interesting, emotive and informative ones – the attitude conveyed in a mood board should successfully reflect the attitude of the collection.

The next step is play with the selected imagery in terms of composition. Without using glue, place your selected images on a board and explore the possibilities of juxtaposition. It is not necessary to fill every bit of space on the board with imagery. Also consider the use of text. This need not mean chunky paragraphs of text. A single word can conjure up an ambience succinctly.

Boards also come in an array of colours besides white, so choose a background that will work best. On the whole neutrals are a better choice – white, black and shades of grey have less of a tendency to jar with the selected imagery. On the other hand, this effect might be exactly what you want.

Top
This mood board has been created for a project on the brand Burberry. It provides a succinct overview of the colour palette and fabric story as well as the historical and contemporary imagery that has inspired the collection.

Bottom
The colours and the fabric embellishments are a focal point of this mood board. These key elements will very likely be integrated in some way into the design development stage and final designs.

Choose two words that inspire you, which can then be developed into two very different concepts. Gather sufficient imagery and fabrics to be able to compile an A3 (11 x 17 in) mood board for each one; 3D objects and text can also be used.

Experiment and explore a range of compositional possibilities. Play. Photograph and rearrange components. Repeat this several times until you are happy with the outcome. Aim to create two very different boards.

The Design Development Process

Design development is a crucial phase in the design process. The links made in the triangulation process between primary and secondary research resources will have elicited a design response, and your sketchbook should contain a good selection of initial design ideas. Initial design ideas are often a quick and spontaneous response to gathered research. The design development process takes place when more consideration is then given to these ideas. This is when you will focus on the development of design details, fabrics, colours, silhouette and proportion.

This phase can take place in a sketchbook or on a layout pad. The translucent pages of a pad make it easy to trace and adapt drawings, which speeds up the process. The pages of a sketchbook do not allow this, but a book lets you house all your research and drawings in one place. Experiment with both options to see which works best for you.

To start the design development process, select the initial ideas that you think are the strongest in terms of design content. Create several variations – anything from 10 to 20 per initial design idea. Experiment by changing various elements such as proportion, fabric, colour distribution, print ideas, hemlines, necklines, sleeves, collars or pockets. It is imperative to remain true to the core concept from one variation to the next and not go off on a tangent.

These rough figure sketches are known as *croquis* drawings (from the French *croquer*, 'to sketch'). Fashion designs are best drawn on a figure as this helps to gauge the balance and proportion of an outfit. Create a template (a pre-drawn figure that designs are added to) for your croquis; this will save you time and allow you to concentrate on the designs.

After this stage, individual garments can be explored further by drawing **flats** (technical/working drawings), which are more explicit and provide more detail.

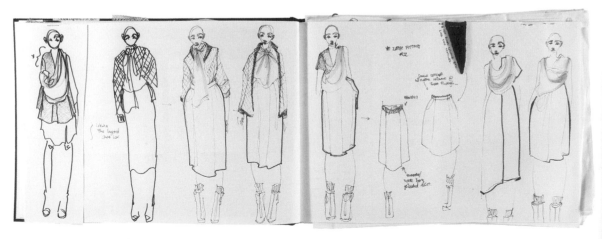

178

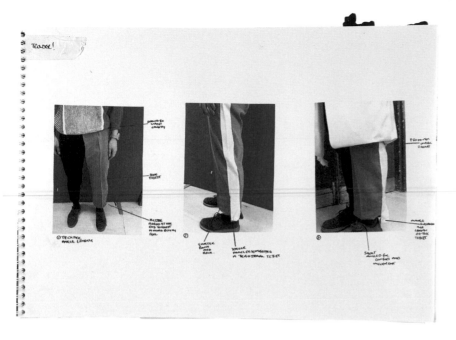

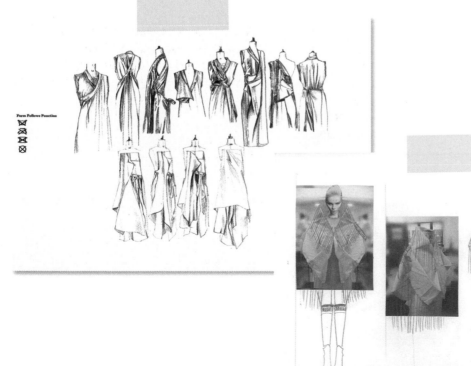

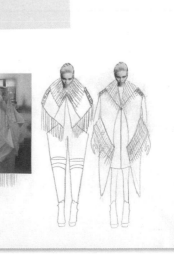

Form Follows Function

Top
The design
development
process can also
take place in 3D.
Whether you are
establishing the
hemline on a pair
of trousers, or
figuring out how the
proportion of one
garment relates to
another, sometimes
there is nothing
better than seeing a
physical version of
an initial design in
front of you.

Centre
This page shows how
a design idea for a
pinafore has been
developed further
through making
changes to design
details and fit.

Bottom
An initial experiment
in calico on a tailor's
dummy has provided
a starting point for
the subsequent
drawn design
developments.

The Portfolio

Your portfolio is a graphic history of your accomplishments; it should demonstrate your design acumen, and drawing, illustration, presentation and technical skills. It is not just a collection of your work, though – it should also reflect your personality.

A design portfolio is usually a ring-bound folder containing plastic display sheets. It can be either A4 (8½ x 11 in) or A3 (11 x 17 in) in size – it is best to try both sizes initially to discover which works for you. Decide on a suitable orientation (either portrait or landscape), and try to be consistent in using only one format or the other when displaying your work. Using a template for each design project will help to make each body of work cohesive and distinct. Double-page spreads make an impact, so try to introduce this element where possible.

A portfolio should be presented in a professional manner, both inside and out. Wipe down the plastic sleeves and the folder itself each time you present your work. Mounted work should be cut and presented straight. The portfolio should express an attention to detail that is evident in the smallest of things.

Portfolios will vary throughout your fashion design career. A student portfolio differs, for example, from a graduate portfolio – the latter being a finer edit of work undertaken during the final year of a degree course or similar programme of study (and sometimes including projects from the penultimate year). It will aim to demonstrate a wide range of skills and a broad knowledge.

Portfolios will also vary depending on the sector of the fashion industry you are working in. An independent designer's portfolio, for example, is a record of collections undertaken as an independent, whereas an industry portfolio is employer-specific, and showcases work undertaken on behalf of a fashion house.

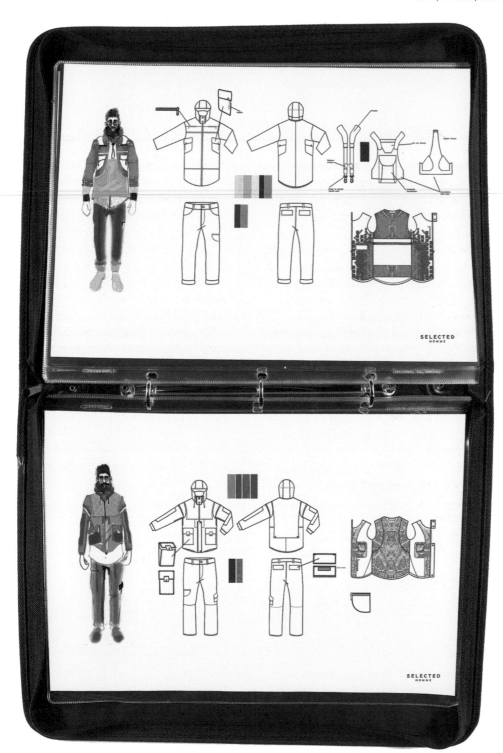

These are finished presentation sheets in a menswear portfolio. This student has considered the layout of the sheets and has dedicated specific areas on the page for the illustration, front- and back-view flats, fabric swatches and outfit details.

Finished Sheets

A portfolio is used to present a fine edit of your research and your **finished sheets**. The finished sheets are the final outcome of a design project, where the edited outfits chosen from the design development stage are illustrated in colour. Each illustrated outfit should be accompanied by flats of front and back views and fabric swatches. It is also useful to provide an illustrated line-up of all the outfits on one page.

These illustrations, as with a mood board, should convey the aesthetic of the collection. So pay special attention to your choice of muse and the position and energy of the pose. If inspiration is needed for creating a contemporary pose refer to current magazines to develop a template. Try and be consistent with your layout per design project to create a cohesive feel.

The Electronic Portfolio

In creating an electronic portfolio, take the same care as you would in putting together a physical portfolio. It is good practice to have both types of portfolio – it will increase the accessibility of your work.

The contents of an electronic portfolio are digitized. An electronic file can be created by using a scanner or by photographing work. Ensure that the work is scanned or photographed at a resolution of at least 300 dpi or ppi (dots per inch or pixels per inch – standard units of measurement for digital image resolution), so that you create imagery of a professional standard. You can also create digital artwork using software from the Adobe Creative Suite – Illustrator, Photoshop and InDesign (as well as others). To ensure that these files are truly accessible to all, save them in a standard electronic format such as PDF (Portable Document Format) or JPEG (a commonly used image file format developed by the Joint Photographic Experts Group).

Many websites showcase graduate work to a wider audience. Arts Thread (www.artsthread.com) provides an interface through which portfolios can be viewed anywhere in the world. Issuu (issuu.com) is another digital publishing platform widely used to showcase work. From a PDF of your work, you can create interactive web documents with links and embedded video. Access to images and downloads on Issuu can be specified by you. Create a fine edit for your online presence – leave the viewer wanting to know more about your work.

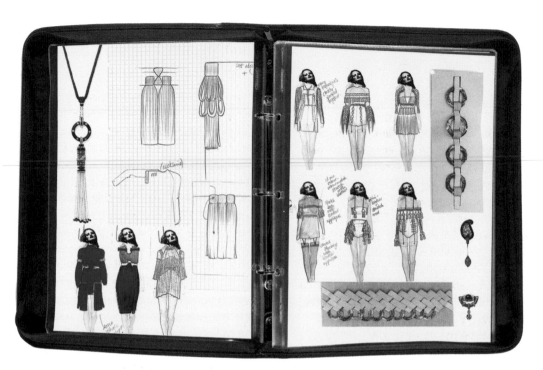

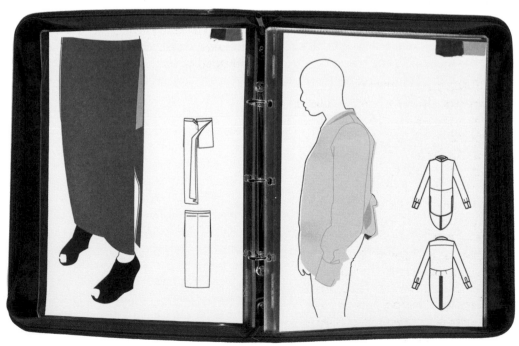

Top
As well as finished sheets, a portfolio should also include an edit of your sketchbook and design development work. By doing this, you help to provide an overview of the project at hand – from research to final product.

Bottom
The spirit of the collection has been carried through into the aesthetic of these final sheets. Graphically pure and simple, these pages have been created using Photoshop and Illustrator.

Makin, the designer behind Makin Jan Ma (MJM) was born and raised in Hong Kong. An eagerness for different life experiences brought him to the UK at the age of 19 to study graphics at Central Saint Martins in London. This degree course emphasized the need to explore and experiment; as a result Makin developed a visual language that is diverse, experimental and deeply personal. As Makin himself reflects, 'When I was studying graphic design I focused on developing a poetic language in visual terms. I think this really affects my approach to creating collections. The process of creating is like writing a poem. Having a graphic design and communications background helps me to use effective methods to communicate with makers and factories.'

A further two years of study at London's Royal College of Art, completing a master's degree in communication and design, introduced Makin to the value of collaborative ventures, setting the tone for future work.

Central to Makin's own artistic endeavours is an emphasis on the conceptual. He also takes advantage of a diverse range of media, which gives him the freedom to translate his many creative ideas into reality. 'It was hard at the beginning when I didn't understand the fashion language very well, but after years of trial and error I have learnt my own language with respects to fashion, which really helps me to communicate fully what I want to express. When I start mixing different media to tell a story, it is fun and exciting.'

The medium of film particularly appeals to Makin. His first film project was a solo venture, with Makin taking charge of the stories, characters and the clothes – an arrangement that created 'a lot of space to create. I think a strong concept helps a designer to be focused when they create. But a good concept leaves space for the creator to wander while creating. Sometimes you do need to get lost along the way in order to search for a deeper meaning.'

This project also established the conceptual approach for his future fashion collections: these collections are built in a way that mirrors the development of a character throughout a film. Makin explains, 'These characters portray very unique personalities that express specific emotions. Emotion is a very interesting part of being human. We all share emotional experiences with each other. By conveying different emotions through imagined characters from varied cultural and social backgrounds, there's a link to society at large. I research the varied behaviours of different cultures and social groups when I invent my characters. So ideally each character is a reflection of a specific consumer demographic. But I don't do this intentionally; it comes about through the process of creating.'

From 2006, Makin's forays into the contemporary fashion scene began to gather interest, and a series of signature MJM prints inspired by stories created by Makin received particular attention. MJM is now sold in the UK, Germany, Belgium, the Middle East, Denmark, France, Italy, the US, Singapore, Hong Kong and Japan.

*Makin Jan Ma's
'Guts Olo' Autumn/
Winter 2012
collection.*

Glossary

additive colour Produced by mixing two or more primary colours of light (red, green and blue).

brief An outline of a task or project designed to inspire you to engage with the project and setting out aims and objectives and a timetable. Student briefs will also contain assessment requirements and criteria.

brainstorm Generating ideas in a group or individually and noting them down on a piece of paper for further exploration. *See also* spider diagram

brand identity Recognizable elements of a brand that distinguish it from others.

carbon footprint The quantity of carbon dioxide emitted when an item is produced.

collage A mixture of diverse materials pasted over a surface to create a composition.

colour forecasters Make predictions based on research about upcoming colour trends for fashion and related consumer products.

colour palette A selection of colours used by a designer in a collection.

complementary colours In the subtractive colour system, colours positioned opposite each other on the colour wheel: red and green, yellow and violet, blue and orange.

copyright A form of legal protection that applies to any medium, typically any original creative idea – artistic, musical and literary works, for example.

croquis A fashion sketch.

cruisewear Also referred to as resort wear; an inter-season, pre-season line of ready-to-wear fashion created by a designer, fashion house or brand in addition to seasonal Spring/Summer and Autumn/Winter collections.

deconstruction The process of taking something apart, whether a garment or a set of pre-established ideas.

demographic A portion of a population. In fashion, a particular group of consumers within the marketplace for whom a designer creates garments.

draping *see* modelling on the stand

eco fashion *see* sustainable fashion

ethnographic research Involves the observation of the interaction of groups of people or individuals in their own environment over a long period of time.

fabric story A group of selected fabrics that best supports your area of research.

fibre A thread of natural or synthetic material that is woven or fused to create a fabric.

finished sheets Presentation sheets, typically composed of coloured fashion illustrations, flats and fabric swatches.

flats Diagrammatic drawings of designs showing all relevant details.

greige goods Undyed and unbleached fabric.

haute couture French for 'high fashion'; bespoke, made-to-measure expensive fashion from a handful of Parisian fashion houses that meet the strict requirements of the Chambre Syndicale de la Haute Couture.

header card A card displaying a fabric sample.

high street fashion Affordable fashion sold at chain stores, both nationally and internationally.

intellectual property Anything that is an intellectual creation – a design, a song, a brand, an invention and so much more.

juxtaposition The placing together of things (images, fabrics, colours, etc.) that contrast.

lead times In magazines, the time needed before the publication date to create an edition/issue. In fashion, the time needed to produce garments from when an order is placed to delivery at various fashion outlets.

light wheel Shows the reaction of light rays and transparent colour in the additive colour system.

macro trend A trend based on a big change in society.

man-made fabric Fabric made from synthetic fibres.

micro trend A trend based on a change in society that is gaining in popularity and building momentum, though having started out as a significantly small movement.

mind map *see* spider diagram

mixed fabric Fabric made when two or more distinct fibres are spun, knitted or woven together.

modelling on the stand Working with fabric on a tailor's dummy.

mood board A board that gives a summary of the inspiration for a collection.

Munsell wheel Shows the interaction of colours created from mixing hues in the partitive colour system.

muse An individual, real or imagined, who inspires a designer, or anyone working in a creative industry, to create. A muse may also represent an ideal consumer, or group of consumers, that the designer is creating garments for.

muslin *see* toile

natural fabric Fabric made from fibres produced by plants, animals or natural processes.

observational drawing Drawing from something that you are directly observing.

partitive colour The mixing of adjacent colours as perceived by a viewer.

pigment wheel Shows the relationship of colours created by mixing primary colours.

prêt-à-porter French for 'ready-to-wear'; fashion that is mass-produced, as opposed to haute couture or bespoke, made-to-measure fashion.

primary colour In the subtractive colour system, a colour that can not be made by mixing other colours. The primary colours are red, yellow and blue.

primary research Original material that you have collected or created. In fashion design, this might include photographs you have taken, sketches you have made and experiments with fabrics and design details.

ready to wear *see* prêt-à-porter

secondary colour In the subtractive colour system, a colour made by mixing different primary colours. The secondary colours are orange (made by mixing red and yellow), green (yellow and blue) and violet (blue and red).

Further Reading

secondary research The collection, review and interpretation of research that already exists, as opposed to primary research. In fashion, you might conduct secondary research by gathering information and images from books, magazines, videos or the internet.

spider diagram A visual system for generating numerous ideas from one main idea. Also called a mind map.

subtractive colour Produced from mixing pigments, dyes, paints, inks and natural colourants.

super-brand A brand that has gained worldwide recognition through its market dominance, customer loyalty and longevity.

sustainable fashion Fashion that is produced with the aim of having as little impact on the environment as possible.

technical drawings *see* flats

tertiary colour In the subtractive colour system, a colour midway between a primary and secondary colour. Tertiary colours are produced by mixing a primary colour with a secondary colour that is adjacent to it on the pigment wheel.

toile A sample of a garment made from inexpensive fabric, typically calico (muslin).

trend The general direction of change or developments. Social, cultural, political and economic influences combine to produce trends.

trend book Books that demonstrate proposed forthcoming trends.

trend forecasting agency An organization that uses fashion intelligence to anticipate forthcoming trends.

triangulation The bringing together of various elements of primary and secondary research to generate design ideas.

Ang, Tom. *Fundamentals of Modern Photography.* London: Mitchell Beazley, 2008.

Armstrong, Tim. *Colour Perception: A Practical Approach to Colour Theory.* Norfolk, UK: Tarquin Publications, 1996.

Atkinson, Jennifer L., Holly Harrison and Paula Grasdal. *Collage Sourcebook: Exploring the Art and Techniques of Collage.* Hove, East Sussex: Apple Press, 2004/Gloucester, MA: Quarry Books, 2005.

Atkinson, Mark. *How To Create Your Final Collection.* London: Laurence King Publishing, 2012.

Black, Sandy. *The Sustainable Fashion Handbook.* London: Thames and Hudson, 2012/New York: Thames and Hudson, 2013.

Brown, Sass. *Eco Fashion.* London: Laurence King Publishing, 2010.

Burke, Sandra. *Fashion Designer: Concept to Collection.* UK: Burke Publishing, 2011.

Carroll, Henry. *Read This if You Want to Take Great Photographs.* London: Laurence King Publishing, 2014.

Craig, Blanche. Collage: *Assembling Contemporary Art.* London: Black Dog Publishing, 2008.

Faerm, Steven. *Fashion Design Course: Principles, Practice and Techniques; The Ultimate Guide for Aspiring Fashion Designers.* London: Thames and Hudson, 2010.

Feisner, Edith Anderson. *Colour.* 2nd edition. London: Laurence King Publishing, 2006.

Fletcher, Kate, and Lynda Grose. *Fashion and Sustainability: Design for Change.* London: Laurence King Publishing, 2012.

Frankel, Susannah. *Visionaries: Interviews with Fashion Designers.* London: V&A Publications, 2005.

Gaimster, Julia. *Visual Research Methods in Fashion.* Oxford and New York: Berg, 2011.

Jennings, Tracy. *Creativity in Fashion Design: An Inspiration Workbook.* New York: Fairchild Books, 2011.

Jones, Sue Jenkyn. *Fashion Design.* 3rd edition. London: Laurence King Publishing, 2011.

Kirke, Betty. *Madeleine Vionnet.* San Francisco: Chronicle Books, 1998.

Leach, R. *The Fashion Resource Book: Research for Design.* London and New York: Thames and Hudson, 2011.

Miglietti, Francesca Alfano. *Fashion Statements: Interviews with Fashion Designers.* Milan: Skira Editore, 2006.

Minney, Safia. *By Hand: The Fair Trade Fashion Agenda.* London: People Tree, 2008/San Francisco: Chronicle Books, 2009.

Penn, Mark J., and E. Kinney Zalesne. *Microtrends: Surprising Tales of the Way We Live Today.* London: Penguin Books, 2008.

Raymond, Martin. *The Trend Forecaster's Handbook.* London: Laurence King Publishing, 2010.

Scully, Kate, and Debra Johnston Cobb. *Colour Forecasting for Fashion.* London: Laurence King Publishing, 2012.

Seivewright, Simon. *Basics Fashion Design 01: Research and Design.* 2nd edition. Lausanne: AVA Publishing, 2012.

Sorger, Richard, and Jenny Udale. *The Fundamentals of Fashion Design.* Lausanne: AVA Publishing, 2006.

Webb, Jeremy. *Creative Vision: Traditional and Digital Methods for Inspiring Innovative Photography.* Lausanne: AVA Publishing, 2005.

Resources

Art Full Text
www.ebscohost.com/academic/art-full-text
A searchable database of articles on fine, decorative and commercial art, as well as photography, folk art, film, architecture and other art-related subjects. Your university library may have a subscription to this database; a free trial is also available.

Fashion Museum, Bath, UK
www.museumofcostume.co.uk
Historic and fashionable dress from the seventeenth century to the present.

Berg Fashion Library
www.bergfashionlibrary.com
An extensive reference source containing texts and images on world dress and fashion throughout history. If your campus library does not have a subscription, there is a 30-day free trail available to institutions, so inform your librarian. There is also a downloadable PDF library recommendation form on the website. If you don't have access through your library, you will need to subscribe as an individual and pay an annual fee.

The Costume Institute, The Metropolitan Museum of Art, New York
www.metmuseum.org/about-the-museum/museum-departments/curatorial-departments/the-costume-institute
Fashionable dress, regional costumes and accessories from around the world, from the fifteenth century to the present.

La Couturière Parisienne
www.marquise.de
Online database of period costume from the Middle Ages to the early twentieth century.

Ethical Fashion Forum
www.ethicalfashionforum.com
The industry body for sustainable fashion.

Fashion-Era
www.fashion-era.com
Website exploring fashion, costume and social history.

Fashion Monitor
www.fashionmonitor.com
Current contacts, news and events in the fashion and beauty industries.

Fashion Net
www.fashion.net
Global fashion portal.

The Future Laboratory
thefuturelaboratory.com
An agency focusing on trend forecasting, consumer-insight research and brand-innovation strategies. The website provides access to the future laboratory blog, and you can also sign up for the newsletter.

Lifestyle News Global
www.lsnglobal.com
Analysis of trends, insights into markets, case studies of products, brands and people, and examination of the inspiration behind design directions in lifestyle industries.

Mintel
www.mintel.com
Mintel is a recognized authority on global market research. Your library will probably have a subscription to this database, due to the importance of understanding the markets. There is also access to a blog on the site that will keep you abreast of relevant issues.

The Museum at FIT, Fashion Institute of Technology, New York
fashionmuseum.fitnyc.edu/
The Museum at FIT has a broad and diverse collection of fashion garments and accessories from the eighteenth century to the present.

Promostyl
www.promostyl.com
A leading trend forecaster. Free access to the Promostyl blog is available on the site. The subjects covered give an insight to the social and environmental happenings that influence trends.

VADS (Visual Arts Data Service)
www.vads.ac.uk/collections
The VADS catalogue provides access to many visual-arts image collections around the UK. All images are freely available and copyright cleared for use in learning, teaching and research in the UK.

The Vogue Archive
http://www.vogue.com/archive
Archive of Vogue magazine from 1892 to today, with full search capability and full-colour images. Your university library may have a subscription to this database; limited access is available to Vogue magazine subscribers.

WGSN
http://www.wgsn.com
Fashion trend forecasting and analysis. You can sign up for the monthly newsletter for free.

Index

Page numbers underlined refer to illustration captions.

189